MW00510130

STOP INSECURITY!

Build Resilience Improving your Self-Esteem and Self-Confidence! How to Live Confidently Overcoming Self-Doubt and Anxiety in Relationship, Insecurity in Love and Business Decision-Making

WRITTEN BY

LEROY REYNOLDS

TABLE OF CONTENTS

COPYRIGHTS

© **Copyright 2020 by** LEROY REYNOLDS

All rights reserved.

This book: STOP INSECURITY!

Build Resilience Improving your Self-Esteem and Self-Confidence! How to Live Confidently Overcoming Self-Doubt and Anxiety in Relationship, Insecurity in Love and Business Decision-Making

WRITTEN BY LEROY REYNOLDS

- From a Declaration of Principles which was accepted and approved equally by a Committee of the American Bar Association and a Committee of Publishers and Associations.

The information provided herein is stated to be truthful and consistent, in that any liability, in terms of inattention or otherwise, by any usage or abuse of any policies, processes, or directions contained within is the solitary and utter responsibility of the recipient reader. Under no circumstances will any legal responsibility or blame be held against the publisher for any reparation, damages, or monetary loss due to the information herein, either directly or indirectly.

Respective authors own all copyrights not held by the publisher.

The information herein is offered for informational purposes solely, and is universal as so. The presentation of the information is without contract or any type of guarantee assurance.

The trademarks that are used are without any consent, and the publication of the trademark is without permission or backing by the trademark owner. All trademarks and brands within this book are for clarifying purposes only and are the owned by the owners themselves, not affiliated with this document.

The vast majority experience frailty or a propensity to need certainty or self-assurance about some part of their lives. For some, sentiments of instability can be settled before they have an enduring and harming sway. However, when it comes to general uncertainty over a long period, the doubts and negative feelings experienced can have a significant effect on life. Insecurity is identified with psychological instabilities like narcissism, nervousness, distrustfulness, and addictive or subordinate characters.

What is Insecurity?

Someone with a high degree of uncertainty can often experience a lack of confidence in many aspects of life. It can be difficult for that person to form long-term relationships or perform daily tasks due to a self-perception of helplessness or failure. Insecurity often causes negative thoughts about a person's ability to equalize peers, achieve goals, or find acceptance and support.

The condition is often accompanied by anxiety: People who experience feelings of anxiety, worry, and self-doubt that characterize anxiety can easily feel powerless to face the challenges of everyday life. Therefore, they may find it easier to resist stressful situations because they feel insufficiently equipped to deal with them.

WHAT CAUSES INSECURITY?

There is not a single cause of insecurity; Many factors can lead to the condition. Insecurity can be the result of a traumatic event, a crisis such as a divorce, bankruptcy, or loss. It can also be the result of someone's environment because unpredictability or discomfort in everyday life can cause anxiety and insecurity about ordinary and routine events. People with recurring uncertainties may also have low self-esteem, experience body image problems, lack of direction in life, or feel ignored by others.

Weakness likewise frequently emerges in grown-ups whose guardians pushed them exorbitantly in youth, regularly because of their folks' craving for progress instead of their own, and in grown-ups whose friends and family impel them to sparkle, regularly at a ridiculous level. Notwithstanding the person's desires or objectives.

The connection bond, or a youngster's first love relationship, shaped with the essential parental figure, additionally assumes a significant job in creating vulnerabilities. An unreliable connection can create when the guardian doesn't react enough to the youngster's needs. A child can build up a shaky connection through maltreatment, just as through straightforward confinement or depression. Kids with conflicting or narrow-minded guardians can grow up on the grounds that they can't make enduring passionate associations and are on the edge and restless, not comprehending what's in store from life, similarly as they didn't have the foggiest idea what's in store from the parent.

Studies have additionally indicated that individuals who submit violence against their partners have experienced insecure attachment as children. Intimate relationships can be another source of uncertainty for many people. People who experience insecurity in their relationships can also be affected by the insecurity of attachment. People in insecure attachment relationships tend to interpret their partner's behavior as hostile or negative. This trend can cause people to react defensively to their partners, which can intensify conflict in the relationship or even cause neutral interaction.

INSECURITY EFFECTS

In addition to struggling to form healthy relationships, insecure people may also have difficulty sharing emotions or being honest about important aspects of everyday life, such as those related to work or school.

A person who is too anxious or insecure to discuss their skills and accomplishments can never receive a promotion, which in turn can cause further uncertainty due to a perceived lack of ability. Insecurity about a person's economy or job stability can also affect mental health and is related to a negative state of mind, hypertension, and other substantial indications.

The individuals who experience issues building connections or meeting others because of constant instability may turn out to be excessively modest or on edge to meet somebody, which can prompt a good way from individuals when all is said in done.

This separation can prompt segregation, which is related to emotional well-being issues like sorrow, social uneasiness, and dementia, just as low confidence. A form of insecurity, also known as social insecurity, can make people feel insecure.

INSECURITY AND MENTAL HEALTH

Insecurity can be seen in a wide variety of mental and personality disorders, including:

- Narcissism

- Schizophrenia

- Borderline personality disorder

- Paranoid personality

- Dependent personality

- Depression

- Anxiety Eating disorders and body image problems.

Deep-seated feelings of fear and uncertainty characterize many of these conditions, although people with these conditions may not seem insecure.

For example, people with a narcissistic personality can boast of accomplishments and abilities, show extreme arrogance, and believe in their superiority. However, these traits often hide deeply hidden feelings of insecurity and doubt.

People with a borderline personality also often experience uncertainties, especially uncertainties related to their sense of identity. People with this personality type may fear abandonment and doubt their own ability to form long-term relationships with other people and therefore become overly dependent on others.

Eating disorders such as anorexia and bulimia, as well as body image problems are closely related to uncertainty.

In the case of eating disorders, uncertainty about a person's appearance or living conditions can play a key role in the development of the condition.

Depression is often associated with low self-esteem. Individuals with low confidence are bound to center and increment their lacks and imperfections, practices that fuel insecurity.

DEALING WITH INSECURITY

People who experience significant uncertainties in everyday life can try to overcome them by identifying the causes.

For example, a man who is afraid to go to work because he thinks he is not performing his daily tasks correctly may wonder what led to that belief and try to find ways to be more positive and realistic about his abilities.

Therapy can also help people who experience significant uncertainties.

A therapist can help people identify and focus on strengths rather than suspected failures.

Insecurity therapy can include cognitive-behavioral techniques, such as talking or writing about someone's insecurities.

Addressing uncertainties in therapy can help people gain confidence in who they are and in the choices they make.

Whether you're struggling with feelings of insecurity related to a living or mental health condition, the right therapist can help you develop skills for dealing with insecurity.

In today's world, confidence is often shown as strong, independent and knowing yourself. On the other hand, insecurity can be seen as someone shy, timid, or insecure about who they are. Uncertainty manifests itself as someone who retains life out of fear. The battle between uncertainty and trust begins.

Admittedly, this is an exact first glimpse of these two states of being. However, it is not the whole picture. The whole image will look different depending on your situation. We all have our strengths and weaknesses, past pain, and victories. We all have places that we trust and places that we are insecure about. What we can expect is that trust controls our lives and not our uncertainties. Knowing where we are trapped is a great way to start seeing how we can build our confidence and stop feeding our insecurities.

TODAY IN THE WORLD, where bad news travels the world online in seconds, people seem more anxious than ever. For adults and children with A.D.H.D., if worries interfere with everyday life, they increase their distraction or impulsiveness and make things seem worse than they are. By turning your relationship into worry and avoiding the pitfalls of negative thinking, you can successfully manage your anxiety.

Fear can be useful: it prepares our bodies for "fight or flight" responses to real threats, such as avoiding tigers in the jungle. But whether there is a genuine or envisioned concern (you are apprehensive about the new position you applied for, or your kid figures you will pass on in a rainstorm), dread implies that somebody's response is more noteworthy than the circumstance requires.

In these moments of anxiety, the sensitive part of the brain (the limbic system, especially the amygdala), fueled by adrenaline, takes over the thinking part of the brain (the frontal lobe and executive functional capacities). What if they become the worst-case scenario? The good news is that uncertainties are not set in stone. You can exceed 100 percent, no matter how big or small they are.

To do this, you just have to work on yourself and come up with an action plan. But know this: No matter what your insecurity tells you (it's not good enough, dignified enough, pretty enough, blah, blah, blah), we are all inherent enough.

Insecurity vs. Trust - Who are you?

Ask yourself who wins the battle between uncertainty and trust in your life. Who you are Open-minded versus closed-minded when we are insecure, we almost pretend to be wounded animals? Walking through life and trying to protect ourselves from our perceived weaknesses. A confident person can be open about their shortcomings and use them as strength. When you act from a place of safety and trust, you can live transparently. By investing less time and vitality ensuring yourself, you have more vitality to reinforce yourself.

Open to learning versus fear of change when you connect to change and embrace the lessons and experiences of good and bad experiences in that change, you act from a place of trust. You are not afraid of failure because you trust yourself and your abilities. Taking the lessons in all their forms is a powerful way to increase your certainty. The more you gain from your own slip-ups, look for the exhortation of others, or are happy to face challenges, the surer you will be in your capacities. If you are afraid of change, you are holding back from significant growth which is an essential growth to gain confidence.

Authentic versus false

To be authentic is to have confidence. They go hand in hand. You don't have to put on a veil to cover your significance or twist your perspective to meet the desires of other people. You love yourself, and you feel comfortable, and you are not afraid to show it. Yes! Pretending to be someone who does not create insecurity and others can easily feel it. It can be difficult to form healthy relationships because there is a level of trust that can never be achieved with someone who is constantly in control. Everyone knows what it feels like to be with someone who is not really with them. Be brave and practice to be yourself. Do it since you love yourself more than the assessments of others.

Taking risks versus staying in a comfort zone

Taking risks can be scary, but even scarier if you are unsure of your abilities. Trust must grow. It comes back every time you take a risk, learns from a mistake, or step out of your comfort zone. What are your comfort zones? By exploring those areas, a little more, you can discover the uncertainty that lives there. An Insecurity that may be stopping you from your dreams. Build people versus shoot down people.

It seems obvious that an insecure person will bring down other people. This sometimes becomes a bigger problem: snowballs from uncertainty to completely toxic behavior. Uncertainty is fueled and sustained by negativity. You need to support the voice in your head that tells you that you are not good enough. Without negativity, you must take responsibility for your actions, feelings, and future.

You would be forced to build your trust by motivating others and helping them see your good qualities, your trainee exercises self-confidence. You are strong enough to be with someone successful, beautiful, and confident. See the positive in differences versus difference judgment. It is common for someone unsure of judging others harshly.

In case you are dubious about a particular bit of your life, you will wrap up genuinely settling on a choice about others at this moment.

At the point when you are certain, you see the positive qualities in others and need the best for them.

Other people's successes motivate you and bring your personal joy.

We see this playing on sexism, racism, and discrimination. When people are not sure who they are, they are not sure who the others are, and they are hopelessly addicted to finding where they fit.

Decision making versus follower

Safe people are often leaders. They can live their own lives and those of others. Some people indeed get these roles, but most people earn them for their skills. The capacity to show your chief and supporters that you have this in any circumstance. You has confidence that others can easily trust you. Not all followers are insecure. However, if you find yourself trusting in the decisions of others most of the time, you may need to build your confidence in yourself. This is your life, and you should not let others decide how to live it.

Provide validation versus seek validation

Confident people can give compliments and compliments easily. They don't feel compromised by the enormity of others. When you act from an insecure place, you are constantly looking for validation because you can feel a feeling of emptiness and sadness within you. You can't fill that gap yourself, so find others who will do it for you. This can put a great deal of weight on your connections since when others neglect to finish that invalid approval, it can reverse discharge and cause you to feel progressively shaky.

Self-reflection versus self-rejection

Something that people have in common with confidence is their ability to sit internally and think of themselves. These people can ask themselves difficult questions, openly look at the answers, and then use self-development to improve those areas. They enjoy being alone with themselves and with their thoughts. However, uncertainty will manifest itself in many self-rejecting ways. If you act from an insecure place, you can find all kinds of creative ways to avoid the truth about yourself.

Seek help versus try to do everything on your own

Safe people are not afraid to ask for help from others. They feel constrained to gain from others and utilize their abilities to further their potential benefit.

Trust that the abilities of others do not destroy your abilities. But insecure people can protect their abilities.

This means that they receive less advice and help from others. Make them get stuck their way and don't learn new skills.

Reduce anxiety and gain confidence

You can reduce anxiety and gain confidence in your emotions, even in stressful times. I have struggled with anxiety since childhood and found some skills that help reduce anxiety while improving my self-esteem. The skill that I want to share with you has allowed me to feel control when fear invades, and my confidence decreases. It helps me decrease my anxiety and gain confidence. I know it may be impossible to reduce the intrusive and automatic thoughts of fear, but it can be.

You may wind up having a common day, and afterward, out of nowhere, stress or dread sneaks in, and unexpectedly you are in a profound dull gap of dread, self-loathing, stress, humiliation, or the need to show unfortunate conduct. Before the urge dominates or the considerations get excessively serious, follow these tips to lessen the power of uneasiness and keep up your certainty, regardless of whether life gives you a warped ball.

How A.A.A.A.H. Ability works Awareness

Simply become mindful of the incredible inclination that is currently meddling with. Your companion may act as a jolt, however in the event that the genuine test is feeling overpowered by the dread that he will leave you and that you will have no companions, point out you're that. Acknowledge the inclination: Acceptance doesn't imply that you like or affirm of conduct or thought; it just permits your psyche to quit battling the inclination. Obstruction prompts dread and agony, while acknowledgment permits change. State so anyone can hear (or to yourself) the feeling you feel.

Simply naming the emotion can decrease intensity, as your brain moves from the amygdala (the enthusiastic focus of your cerebrum) to the frontal projection where handling and critical thinking happen.

Naming our feelings can give us a basic space from feeling. It implies that we are not simply that feeling.

Furthermore, it additionally advises us that feeling is impermanent. At the point when we recall that we are greater than we feel at that point, we can find a sense of contentment with the inclination and essentially tune in to what that feeling is attempting to let us know.

Action: What are some actions you can take to reduce the intensity of this emotion and/or fix the problem for now? That can mean distracting yourself from the situation, focusing on something you have control over, or taking a break from doing something you enjoy.

Evaluate: Evaluate possible outcomes before taking action. Are there actions that don't solve the problem, but that helps you feel more in control, happy, or safe? Are there negative side effects of taking this action?

How intense is your concern or drive now?

The "H" asks you to register and see if the intensity has decreased and how much control or clarity you have obtained. Although you may not have solved the problem, you have probably reduced the intensity of your thought or drive. A significant point to recall is that we can indeed control a limited amount of much throughout everyday life. I realize that I may not be able to solve all the problems that concern me, but I can take control if I respect my emotions and try to solve the problem. You can also do this by trying these five steps to reduce anxiety and increase your confidence.

How to regain your confidence after fear?

Anxiety and confidence: how do they relate to each other? In my job as a life coach, many of my clients tell me that because they live with higher than normal levels of anxiety, they feel that their self-confidence has been undermined. This makes sense because living with a high degree of fear makes us feel limited, doubting ourselves, and our abilities.

This sense of limitation decreases our self-confidence, which only increases feelings of anxiety, as we feel less confident in our ability to deal with anxiety situations. But there is hope. We do not have to stay in this cycle. Here are some ways to regain your confidence after fear.

1. Access where you are and where you need to Now begin asking yourself, where might you rate your certainty level at 10? (10 is high, and one is low). It is important to be compassionate and not judge your responses. Then imagine what a higher level of self-confidence looks like. What could you do with more confidence? Write some examples of behaviors, habits, and feelings that your self-confidence would have. Feel excited because you know that more confidence is not only possible, but you deserve it.

2. Challenge yourself to act. Use your vision of self-confidence to inspire you, take action, and lovingly challenge yourself. When my self-confidence came to an end after fear, I was afraid of meeting people I knew, of being caught off guard, and of having to talk.

Aware of this, one day, I challenged myself. Every day for 30 days, I went to the busy local supermarket where there was always a great opportunity to see someone I knew. If you knew someone, you would have to say "hello" and talk. Part of me was scared. Part of me was excited. By day 30, my confidence had grown tremendously as I had gone to my fears instead of turning away from them. Make sure to begin little, and as your certainty develops, so will the size of the difficulties.

3. Become a cheerleader yourself. Get used to praising yourself. Stand in front of a mirror every night before bed, look yourself in the eye and congratulate yourself (out loud or out loud) on something you did well that day. Announce your price. Become a cheerleader for yourself. When you notice feelings of anxiety that are to be expected as your comfort and confidence zone increases, calm

down by saying, "I can do this." You may want to write a list of other phrases, statements, or "strength." thoughts' that you want to tell you all day. You can even set silent alarms on your phone, so you can read these powerful words.

4. Concentrate on setting off the "rest and absorption" reaction During 'fight or flight,' our sympathetic nervous system helps us deal with the threat by increasing our heart rate, breathing, furthermore, pulse. When our psyche feels the risk has been evacuated, our circulatory strain, heart, and breathing come back to ordinary, our muscles unwind and procedures, for example, absorption continues, halting during the 'battle or flight.' This is because of the parasympathetic sensory system or the 'rest and processing' response, which reestablishes harmony in the body.

5. Make an effort not to be hesitant to demand help. Remember: you are not the only one. Offer your considerations, emotions, and difficulties with loved ones and request their help. They will likewise need you to feel more secure once more. There are bolster gatherings, on the web and disconnected, for individuals on a similar excursion as you who need to reestablish their certainty after dread. There are moreover arranged specialists who can help you with understanding the establishments of fear and offer mechanical assemblies to help you with feeling increasingly invigorated when life gets horrendous.

People always say that when you find the right person, it all makes sense, and all doubts disappear. People also say relationships cost work, and not all rays of the sun and rainbows shoot unicorns. Where do these two ideas come together? If you question your relationship in any way, is that always a bad sign? To learn how to reduce uncertainty, you must first understand your self-esteem. Self-confidence begins early in life.

Low self-esteem is the product of their education and life experiences and manifests itself in the loss of confidence, self-esteem, and confidence. Feelings of uncertainty are learned during our journey when you (poorly) learn through negative experiences to connect negative events with rejection. For example, when you are a child, you learn to feel insecure if you are raised by caregivers who participate in inconsistent parenthood. This happens when the disciplines of your parents or caregivers are disciplined inconsistently.

This inconsistency stems from the fact that parenting depends on mood, rather than constantly relying on certain rules, standards, or expectations. At school, this inconsistency is often emphasized in friendships. Children go through so many hormonal and emotional changes at school that emotional reactions and hurt feelings occur daily, if not weekly. If you were taught to see these changes simply as emotional and not personal, your self-esteem would remain intact.

However, children often internalize these daily rejections so that they are not pleasant or unwanted. Even after children put on makeup (which also happens daily), they may be left with the scars of possible rejection. Children then learn early on how to "walk on eggshells" to avoid being rejected again.

Examples of how doubt can manifest are the following:

- A good friend gets mad when you have to say "no" to do something with her for whatever reason

- Your accomplice shouts at you each time he is worn out, or focused mother in her mother's group opposes any opinion she has about parenting.

- Someone close to you will ignore you if you are in a group

- Your partner x cheats on you, so you become paranoid, any partner will cheat on you in the future

Reduce doubts and concerns with important people in your life. The preceding points emphasize negative behavior that can lead to fear of rejection.

Each of these examples highlights the behavior of others, mistakenly internalized as their fault. However, this internalization was incorrect. The examples above would be better internalized as external responses due to the other person's problems. Let's take a quick look at each example:

A good friend gets angry

This is a reflection of your friend's problems and has nothing to do with your behavior. You also have the right to say 'no' when you are busy.

Your partner yells at you

Your state of mind dictates their reactions to you.

Your mood is the problem, not your behavior.

A mother in your mother group is arguing against you

This is a reflection of the mother, who is intimidated by her opinion or insecure about her role within the group. You have the right to have a different opinion than hers.

Your good friend will ignore you in a group

This is a mistake, or overcompensating the other person for their insecurities or jealousy, by focusing on those who may need more work to turn out to be dear companions or family.

Your partner x is cheating on you

This is a reflection of your partner x and does not affect you. Regardless of what happens in the relationship, the deception is only the fault of the person who engages in the behavior.

The five best answers to reduce anxiety in your partner

1. Restore your confidence to make sure you have the strength to cope when something goes wrong and to be resistant to negative experiences

2. Honestly asking if someone's behavior reflects their problems (not yours)

3. Trust yourself and your instincts

4. Be open and honest with loved ones, share your feelings, and question inappropriate behavior.
5. Live in a world of facts, not perception. Therefore, you only act on your concerns if you are 100% sure that your judgment is correct (ask if it is necessary before acting, for example).

The main thing is to believe that uncertainty is not a healthy emotion which leads to negative and destructive behavior. It is not your fault that you feel this way, but as an adult, you have the option of continuing to feed yourself or challenge this and overcome it. By doing the latter, you will enrich your relationships, enhance your career, and live a much healthier, happier, and more successful life.

Fear and relationships: how to stop stealing magic

Intimate relationships reflect and reflect the best and worst of us all. They can fuel our battles or quiet them. At the point when they are correct, they feel mysterious. Regardless of whether they are correct, dread can take enchantment and extricate the association between two individuals who have a place together. All connections require trust, delicacy, persistence, and weakness. People with anxiety often have these with the truck and will give generously to the relationship. The problem is that sometimes fear can erode them just as quickly.

If you are someone who is struggling with fear, many things about you make it easy to love yourself. All relationships struggle sometimes, and when fear is at stake, struggles can be very specific, very normal, and specific. Nervousness can work inquisitively and will influence various connections in an unexpected way, so not the entirety of coming up next are applicable to each relationship. Here are a few different ways to fortify and shield your relationship from the impacts of dread:

Supplement passionate assets.

You are presumably very touchy to the necessities of others and give an open and rich relationship to your relationship. Sometimes, however, fear can get those resources out of the relationship as quickly as you invest them. This is fine, there is enough to love you to make up for this, but it can mean making sure those resources are replenished whenever you can, wait for your partner with attention, gratitude, affection,

affection, a lot of affection, and a conversation around him.

Show your partner support as well.

Your partner may be reluctant to "overwhelm" you with worries, especially if those worries don't seem to be as great as the ones you have. People with fear are so strong, and it is impossible to live without fear, so make sure your partner knows that no matter how big or small their fight is, sometimes you can be the follower. Partners of anxious people may tend to ignore their concerns, but this may mean allowing them to feel nurtured and supported by you, which would be a great loss to both of you. Sometimes also consider the rock. Ask, wait, touch. There is nothing more healing than the warmth of the person you love.

Let your partner know what you think.

Anxious thoughts are extremely personal, but let your partner in. It is an important part of intimacy. You will often think about what you need to do to feel safe, what makes you feel bad, and what can go wrong. You will also have a tremendous ability to think about other people, anxious people do, but be sure to get involved in the thoughts that are arresting you. Keeping things too much for yourself increases the distance between two people.

Asking for quiet is fine, but not too much.

Fear can infiltrate anything. If not controlled, it can leave you questioning things that don't deserve to be questioned, like your relationship. It is perfectly fine, and it is very normal to ask your partner for calm. Too much, though, and you may feel like you need it. Necessity is the enemy of desire and can smother the spark over time. Make sure that your partner has the opportunity to love you spontaneously, without being asked: it is good for them and even better for you.

Be vulnerable.

Anxiety can affect relationships in several ways. In some people, it can create a need for constant peace of mind. In other cases, it can make them stop, making them less vulnerable to possible penalties. Vulnerability, being open to others, is beautiful and is the essence of successful and healthy relationships.

The problem with overprotecting yourself is that it can trigger rejection against the one you are trying to protect yourself against.

Part of intimacy is leaving someone closer than the rest of the world. Trust that person with the vulnerable, messy, and brave parts of you: the parts that are often beautiful, sometimes mind-blowing, and always in order with the person who loves them.

It is understandable to worry about what can happen if someone has open access to these parts of you, but see those concerns for what they are, concerns, not realities, and trust what happens when it opens. By loving and being loved, you will be fine because you will be.

Be careful when projecting fear into your relationship.

Anxiety can't be caused by anything, in particular, that's one of the terrible things about it, so you're going to be looking for a target, an anchor to keep it still and make sense.

If you are in an intimate relationship, the target is there, drawing your fear to its gravity. This can provoke feelings of doubt, jealousy, suspicion, and uncertainty.

Fear can be a villain. That doesn't mean your relationship is worth your fear, most likely not, but your relationship is important, relevant, and often in your mind, making it too easy a goal.

Recollect that it doesn't imply that you need to stress since you stress. Weight if you have to, yet then recognize the truth about it: fear, not the truth. You are loved, and you are afraid, and you are doing well. Let that be the truth you have.

Investigation prompts loss of motion.

There is a truism: "Examination prompts loss of motion" since it is. "Is it love? Or, on the other hand, desire? Or on the other hand, am I joking? Consider the possibility that my heart breaks into little, barbed pieces. By what means will it work in the event that we don't care for a similar music/books/nourishment/motion picture? Consider the possibility that we book get-away and carrier interferes. Imagine a scenario where one of us becomes ill.

Consider the possibility that we both become ill. Imagine a scenario in which we can't get a discount. Or, on the other hand, pay the home loan? Imagine a scenario in which he becomes weary of me. "Indeed. I realize you know how it sounds.

What you center around is the thing that gets significant, so in the event that you center around potential issues, they will invest your vitality until they are sufficiently enormous to mess up you. They will drain your vitality, your feeling of delight, and your capacity to move. You most likely realize that, yet what can be done. Here's something you can attempt ... Set a time allotment where you can imagine there is no reason to worry. In this way, for instance, stress over 10-3 consistently, and afterward, inhale, let go, and imagine you're alright. You don't need to trust it, "imagine." Tomorrow you will have another chance to stress if vital. Leave yourself alone guided by the proof, not the stresses that frequent you at 2 am.

Come, nearer, don't go.

At the point when you center around everything about, gets unsteady. You can concentrate on things that are not directly with your accomplice or your relationship, while simultaneously looking for affirmation that your accomplice cherishes you and is submitted. This may lead you to push your accomplice away ("You frustrated me") and afterward attract her to you ("Tell me you love me. You love me, right?").

Visit with your accomplice, and if it's a known procedure, give a sheltered path to your accomplice to reveal to you when it's going on. Concur on how it will look. At the point when it occurs, ensure you don't hear it out as a basic, it's not, it's your accomplice who requests dependability with the manner in which they love one another.

Troublesome discussions can bring you closer.

All connections experience troublesome things every now and then, yet dread can make things more undermining and greater than they are. The allurement might be to abstain from conversing with your accomplice about troublesome issues since you are worried about what the relationship may do to him. Troublesome issues don't leave - they replicate until they arrive at breaking point. Trust that you and your accomplice can deal with a troublesome conversation. Connections depend on trust and trust that your relationship can experience troublesome discussions.

Tell your accomplice what it resembles to be you.

People are mind-boggling animals, and we approach somebody, and their history, regardless of whether it is somebody who has been with you for some time, is the spirit of closeness. Individuals change, stories change, and even in close connections, it's anything but difficult to put some distance between the individual who nods off around evening time. Tell your accomplice what your dread of you is. Discussion about your considerations, how dread influences you, your activity, your relationship, your accomplice, and how appreciative you are for adoration and backing.

Tell your accomplice what triggers you.

Is there a specific circumstance that will result in general set your dread of fire? Groups? Outsiders? Trouble leaving? Boisterous music in the vehicle? To be late? Converse with your accomplice so that on the off chance that you are in the circumstance all of a sudden, the person in question comprehends what is befalling you.

Show restraint.

The snappy arrangement can't the best.

As an approach to feel much improved and facilitate your nervousness, you might be enticed to locate a fast answer for an issue or issue in your relationship. You might be disappointed with your accomplice's craving to pause or defer some activity, or your protection from continue discussing it, however, be available to the way that your accomplice may see things in an unexpected way, once in a while more plainly. Try not to inhale, talk, and accept your accomplice is taking the time or pulling back from the discussion because of the absence of duty or on the grounds that the issue can't be sufficient.

Ensure you take great consideration of yourself.

Being enamored is insane. However, it can occupy you from dealing with yourself and dealing with somebody uncommon. We all in all will, as a rule, do this, yet for those with nervousness, it very well may be especially inconvenient on the grounds that once you're out of parity, the wrinkle can fix different things. Dealing with yourself is significant.

Eating right (a sound eating routine wealthy in omega 3s, low in starches, and handled sugars), just as ordinary exercise and reflection, build up the mind from nervousness. In the event that is dealing with yourself is narrow-minded, consider it along these lines:

It's not reasonable to anticipate that your accomplice should bolster you through your dread on the off chance that you don't do all that you can to help yourself. Consider individual consideration as an interest in you, your relationship, and your accomplice. Additionally, recall that anything useful for nervousness is useful for everybody, so converse with your accomplice about finding a solid way of life together: cooking, working out, and thinking together ... fun.

Comprehend that your accomplice needs constrain

To keep your relationship close, solid, and associated, your accomplice's manufactured limits can be incredible. Comprehend that limits are not how your accomplice fends you off, yet rather as an approach to shield yourself from 'getting' your dread. You might be concerned and need to discuss something again and again. However, that is not really bravo, your accomplice, or your relationship. Your accomplice can adore you and draw an intense underline between the last time you talk about something and whenever you need it.

Talking is solid, yet discussing something very similar again and again can be debilitating and make an issue where there is none. Realize that your accomplice adores you, and that limits are imperative to support cherish and develop the relationship, not to conflict with it. Converse with your accomplice about what you have to feel great in spite of your dread.

Welcome Limits - It will help keep your association solid and cherishing and will cause your accomplice to feel equipped for keeping up a feeling of self without stressing over your interests. Stresses are infectious, so if your accomplice (in the long run) needs to draw a line around their interests, get it going: it will help save the enthusiastic assets of the relationship and will be useful for both of you.

Chuckle together

This is significant! Chuckling is a characteristic counteract to the pressure and strain related to tension. Chuckling together will fortify the bond among you, and if a few days (weeks, months, or months) have been upsetting, it will help you both recollect why you began to look all starry eyed at one another. Dread can cause you to overlook that life ought not to be paid attention to.

In the event that it's been excessive since a long time ago, your accomplice saw the state of your face when you grin (which will be delightful and most likely one reason they went gaga for you in any case), discover an explanation, an enjoyable one. Motion pictures, recollections, YouTube ... everything.

From the rapture of understanding that somebody delightful is moved by you as much as you are by him, to the anguish of uncertainty and conceivable misfortune, to the security, riches and, some of the time, the quiet of more profound love, closeness is a vehicle for every conceivable feeling Fear influences connections, yet by being available to its effect and responding purposely, you can ensure your relationship and make one that is solid, solid, and flexible.

Basic reasons for dread were seeing someone.

Connections are as well as can be expected: be sensational, with bunches of snickers and late-night discussions and eccentric dates. In any case, they can, in like manner, be significant wellsprings of nervousness and stress, and there are, in reality, some basic reasons for relationship uneasiness.

While realizing that your nervousness triggers a relationship may not resolve emotions all alone, it's in every case great to distinguish an issue in light of the fact that once you recognize what's happening, it can change things.

All things considered, I addressed 15 love and relationship specialists about the things they find in their everyday rehearse that frequently inspire extraordinary dread and nervousness seeing someone, and what they can do in the event that they see a portion of these issues in their own affiliation. There appear to be some challenging things that can trigger excruciating sentiments regardless of what else you have in a relationship, including things like cash, dread of dismissal, dread of surrender, and so forth. Turns out, becoming hopelessly enamored by and large can be too upsetting! Here are 15 reasons for dread seeing someone so you can distinguish what's going on in your own life.

1. Become hopelessly enamored

"Relationship uneasiness changes," Dawn Maslar, otherwise called "the adoration scientist," tells Bustle. "A couple will feel increasingly on edge toward the start of dates." It vanishes with time. "Nervousness diminishes significantly when you experience passionate feelings for," she says.

One that you distributed with somebody; you unwind. "Some portion of the mind, the amygdala, which is liable for enrolling uneasiness, is deactivated when two or three experiences passionate feelings," she says. Truly like this! "Be that as it may, this deactivation is transitory, and the dread may return following a year or two." Oh, damn it.

"The best reason for dread gets powerless against another person," she says. "We have serious issues, one for security and one for adoration." But security and love can be totally the equivalent. All things considered, "in a relationship, you can travel every which way" between feeling that you need to remain safe and feel that you can leave yourself alone cherished, particularly if you have been hurt already. Go moderate, and in the event that you have a sense of security, permit yourself to feel everything.

2. Cash

"Cash is one of the main sources of relationship dread," New York-based relationship master and writer April Masini told Bustle. "Individuals are not typically legit about cash until there is an issue." And then it is past the point of no return.

"It could be the revelation of contrariness in sparing and spending or a shrouded loss of work, and individuals are embarrassed about this kind of misfortune, or a concealed financial balance or customary costs," he says. In any case, it is appalling.

Likewise, numerous couples believe that adoration outperforms everything until they wed the devastated artist and understand that the expense of supplanting the high temp water evaporator is constraining them and that the ruined artist, they love appears to be a daily practice without a genuine activity... 'says Masini. "Things change. Cash seeing someone is steady. Treat it or alarm it."

3. Envy

"Envy is one of the fundamental drivers of dread seeing someone," life mentor Kali Rogers told Bustle. "Envy is because of the absence of certainty, and the absence of certainty is common because of low confidence." To expand your confidence, and you will have a superior possibility of staying away from it. "In principle, the ideal approach to take a shot at envy is to build up your own confidence," says Rogers. Practically speaking, it works!

4. Indeed, genuinely: desire

[Jealousy] draws out our greatest instabilities and can transform a sound relationship into a lethal reality in a matter of seconds," affirmed relationship mentor Rosalind Sedacca tells Bustle. "The envious accomplice is overpowered by the dread that anticipates and fears the most noticeably awful." Instead of accepting the best, they generally look for the most exceedingly awful conceivable result.

"The motivation behind the desire is to safeguard the guards and ask them to continually legitimize their conduct," she says. "The outcome is a foreboding shadow over the relationship that will influence the two accomplices. Desire ought to be tended to through treatment or preparing except if it is shown that it is objective and is tended to in like manner. "Also, if envy is truly founded on realities, well, that is a totally extraordinary issue.

5. The dread o losing love.

There is a well-known confusion that regularly comes up seeing someone: "In case I'm not ____, the individual in question will never again cherish me," analyst Erika Martinez tells Bustle. "It's a typical thing that I regularly hear in my office, and it keeps individuals on their brains, so they don't focus on their accomplices or appreciate connections." Danger zone. By focusing on your accomplice and making the most of your relationship, you guarantee that both your accomplice and your relationship are solid and cheerful.

6. The dread of relinquishment.

"One of the fundamental drivers of dread in a relationship is dread of dismissal or dread of deserting," says Darren Pierre, instructor, speaker, and writer of The Invitation to Love: Recognize the Gift Despite the Pain, the

Bustle dread and obstruction. "Our own vulnerabilities are frequently reflected by our accomplices." It is ordinary to be worried about such things, however, as opposed to staying discreet, talk about it.

"Rather than permitting those vulnerabilities to startle dread, call those things on your accomplice so they can bolster you in the development spaces that are accessible to you," he says.

8. The dread of dismissal.

"A large portion of the contentions about envy, family, work, online life, and cash depends on dismissal," Zen psychotherapist and neuro marketing strategist Michele Paiva told Bustle. The basic dread during these fights is that they are straight dismissed.

For example, in case you have a warmed discussion about what measure of time you proceed with his sister or him and his mates, it's "the reason not want to contribute that vitality with me? "She says. "Dismissal is our inclination, yet our conduct that follows is safeguard or resistance; when we unwind in our connections, we feel less dismissed, and that is the reason we guard ourselves or the restriction demonstrations." The more you can be available and loose in your relationship, the more joyful you will be. Be that as it may, if the dread is right, react. "I am a Zen specialist, so I center around inviting trepidation," she says.

"In the event that you thump on the entryway, you can open the entryway, converse with her, see her, inhale and close the entryway realizing that you are cognizant. Try not to open the entryway, welcome her, and make espresso. She is there to keep you alert, not to be your companion. '

9. Ex correspondence

"One of the primary drivers of relationship uneasiness is ceaseless correspondence with an ex," creator, life strategist, and speaker Carey Yazeed tells Bustle. "This makes dread as well as lead outrage and eventually, a separation." Not Good "On the off chance that you have to speak with your ex, disclose to the new individual you are dating why correspondence is important." What's more, in case you don't have to, don't do it, especially in case it makes your current boo bothersome.

Regardless of our endeavors to all the more likely to comprehend and defeat our relationship tension, it might be very difficult to do it in segregation. In case you experience any issues during your relationship adventure, consider searching for the assistance of a good counselor who can work with you to develop a guide.

I trust these devices are helpful in investigating and managing the remarkable fear that can break out in wistful associations. Despite the way that it is a maxim, review that the huge relationship we have with ourselves is.

It is basic to stay inquisitive when the nervousness of our relationship is stirred and to all the more likely comprehend the cause of our feelings of dread. This will assist us with being increasingly mindful and with building up an away from self. By understanding our own considerations, feelings, and needs and imparting them to our accomplices, we can at last feel increasingly associate, and in this manner, more settled.

Instability in a relationship can be hard to deal with, particularly if your accomplice can't get it and is simply infatuated with confounding agony. Discover how to conquer relationship vulnerabilities and have a superior relationship.

Experiencing passionate feelings can feel like a luxurious situation.

Regardless, if you find that your love can't rapidly, you may hurt yourself or feel problematic about the state of the relationship. Cognizance and overseeing helplessness in a relationship can't, especially if your assistant doesn't get you or what you are encountering.

What's more, in some cases, the disarray in the degrees of closeness between two sweethearts can cause more torment and dissatisfaction than even a separation. The division is a solitary advance that finishes the end. In any case, a shaky relationship causes you to accept that you are infatuated, but you feel that you have just isolated.

Weakness in a relationship

Is it true that you are encountering an unreliable relationship now? For what reason do you truly feel uncertain in your relationship? Probably the ideal approach to comprehend relationship frailties is to comprehend the wellspring of the issue. You are unreliable in light of the fact that you fear to lose your adored one (maybe to someone else). Regardless, for what reason do you feel subsequent?

To truly comprehend the vulnerabilities of connections, you should consider your vulnerabilities and locate the genuine explanation. What's more, above all, is there anything your accomplice can do about it?

Converse with your accomplice.

At the point when you appreciate the explanation behind weakness in your relationship, banter with your associate about it. You don't have to tell your assistant that you feel questionable, which can simply additionally strain the relationship.

Basically, express that periodically, you don't feel appreciated and explain a couple of models when you feel problematic. Make an effort not to sound puzzled or hopeless, essentially state business. In case your accessory worships you, they endeavor to calm you down and cause you to feel much improved.

Be that as it may, before raising your vulnerabilities, ensure this is something your accomplice can sensibly change. You can request that your beau give more consideration to you when he is with his companions or to converse with another young lady. It's not alright to request that he quit conversing with the young ladies or their companions!

Improve?

When you express your vulnerability about your relationship, you can feel much improved. Regardless, in case you feel problematic, altogether after your accessory changes his direct or consoles you, you are on an uncertain surface. From one viewpoint, your accomplice may think he is doing a major issue out of the blue and will keep on doing the things that cause him to feel shaky.

Then again, your accomplice can change or console you. However, you can't be persuaded regardless of what your accomplice says or improves the relationship itself. Vulnerability in a relationship can emerge for the most evident reasons, yet the most widely recognized reasons are the point at which you imagine that your accomplice is unreasonably bravo or you believe that there are such a large number of individuals around you who are greatly improved. At that point, you (and possibly take from your accomplice).

Step by step instructions to feel unreliable in a relationship

In the event that you feel uncertain in the relationship, much after your accomplice has changed his method for representing you and consoles you, you may simply be better with yourself. Furthermore, comprehend that your accomplice can't issue, you do!

Your assistant is a bit of your life.

Leave your accomplice alone a piece of your life, not your entire life. It's as straightforward as that. At the point when your life rotates around your affection life, it's anything but difficult to get fixated on it and pick little nonexistent defects that don't exist. What's more, instabilities can emerge when you need to converse with your accomplice or constantly meet her. Carry on with your own life and devote some portion of it to cherish. It will keep your adoration life progressively fun and energizing, and you will be less worried about weaknesses in the relationship.

Trust your accomplice

Except if you have entered the relationship without truly knowing whether your accomplice likes you definitely, you should make sense of how to trust in your associate. Both are pulled in to each other and love each other, so why scrutinize or find ways to deal with get your associate in the demonstration? Make sense of how to accept your assistant aside from on the off chance that you have strong inspirations to address them.

Invest energy with your partners

Contribute vitality with your own social affair of sidekicks and have some great occasions. It causes you in two unique manners. To begin with, you will comprehend that a relationship can't by investing energy with companions. Two: on the off chance that you watch somebody on various occasions, you truly don't undermine your accomplice!

Be hopeful

Stop cynicism. Quit asking yourself what to do if your accomplice leaves you or what your darling does in the event that they go out without you. Your accomplice became hopelessly enamored with you as a result of the superb individual you are, recollect that. In the event that you ever feel uncertain in the relationship, figure out how to manage it by conversing with your accomplice, or survey the circumstance by imagining your accomplice's perspective.

Increment your certainty

One of the most evident yet humiliating explanations behind vulnerability in a relationship is an absence of trust. It harms, yet it's valid. You are uncertain on the grounds that you think you are sufficiently bad.

Exchange a couple of looks with a cutie when you go out with companions, pick a few leisure activities and periodically compel yourself to accomplish something you've for the longest time been tingling to do, whether or not it's outside your standard scope of nature. The more you drive, the all the all the more driving experience you will have.

Moreover, the more you figure out how to carry on with your life without limit, the more you will figure out how to pick up trust in yourself, and you're justified, despite all the trouble.

Like yourself

Instabilities in a relationship show up when you are glad to see your accomplice, however, not so much content with what you find in your claim reflect. Go out routinely and start dressing like a million bucks. Furthermore, practice and get the fantasy body you constantly needed. In the event that you feel like a million dollars, you know your worth somebody.

What's more, on the off chance that you have a sense of security and stately, relationship frailties have no place else to go yet waste!

Settle on a choice about your vulnerabilities.

Not all connections are impeccable at this point. In some cases, it tends to be sheltered and appealing. However, you can, at present, feeling shaky. Your accomplice can underestimate you, play with others, or even totally disregard you. On the off chance that you are shocked by vulnerability about the relationship, significantly in the wake of conversing with your accomplice about it, and considerably subsequent to changing with the certainty building tips recorded here, at that point, something isn't right.

Perhaps your accomplice just underestimates it and doesn't generally try helping you rest easy thinking about the relationship.

At the point when confronted with such a circumstance, where the vulnerability in a relationship can't lead to an absence of trust yet to an absence of affection and an overdose of carelessness, the time has come to settle on a choice.

Being caught in a shaky relationship is more awful than saying a final farewell to your accomplice or cheating. The vulnerability in a relationship will remove certainty and satisfaction from your life, and you will never feel genuinely adored. You simply wilt from the back to front until the relationship closes.

1. Quit believing it's about you.

An egocentric perspective guarantees that you pursue the curve qualities where they don't exist. In case your assistant doesn't want to go out, don't accept that this is a direct result of you that he could have had an awful day at work simply, making them lose their vitality.

Quit psychoanalyzing each word decision your accomplice makes and be progressively present at the present time so you can see the message behind your tone, physical nearness, and demeanor. Being fixated on concealed implications is a certain method to overlook the main issue.

Try not to censure your accomplice for being excessively peaceful or continually ask, "What do you think?" Every Conversation A mind-boggling desire to fill each second of quiet with pointless words is a propensity for an unreliable individual. Take your accomplice's hand, breathe in, breathe out, and partake in the quietness together. Who says you don't care for being as one without words?

2. Quit psyching yourself.

Your musings can be the closest companion or the most noticeably terrible adversary of your relationship. The idea of your thoughts legitimately influences the idea of your relationship. Have you at any point had negative musings like "I know some time or another they'll make me debilitated" or "How might they love me?" These considerations have little to do with the real world; however, a lot to fear. At the end of the day, the issue you're worried about doesn't exist - you caused it to up!

3. Quit conveying such baggage.

Have you anytime been in such a ghastly relationship, that you simply need everything, so you don't need to reconsider it? Join the club. It will be hard to track down somebody who doesn't have gear since this adoration is an unusual (and here and there rough). A little stuff is fine. However, you ought to relieve your burden before beginning another relationship. Disregard any staying destructive emotions that may wait and understand that your new relationship is another opportunity to desert the entirety of that.

The excellence of life: you can begin the same number of times again as vital!

4. I quit seeing things clearly.

How would you respond when somebody censures you for something you believe can't blame? The survey says: You get cautious. Thus, going up against your accomplice about an issue, regardless of how evident it might be, can trigger a cautious reaction. This, for the most part, prompts an extended, brought down fight that is something contrary to profitable, as both are too occupied to even consider demonstrating that they have the motivation to determine their contention.

If you have an issue, don't point your finger quickly, notwithstanding, approach your gather as one with compassion and cognizance. Have certainty that none of you are absolutely "right" or "wrong." The authentic answer is somewhere in the middle.

5. Stop feeling jittery about nothing.

Let's face it: we, in general, speak with people of the other sexual orientation. Since a child and a youngster (or a child and a child or a youngster and a youngster) are sidekicks doesn't infer that more things happen.

Keep away from the compulsion to see your accomplice's telephone, Face book messages, or email account. While this may briefly quiet your nerves in the event that you don't see anything, it likewise conducts that can immediately get addictive, also harm to trust in the relationship when they find Big Brother is viewing.

6. Quit putting off ungainly discussions.

While the struggle is distressing for your momentary relationship, it will reinforce the quality of your long-haul relationship. Confronting your issues valiantly can assist you with drawing nearer to your accomplice. Never joke around, and you will create certainty so solid that you can mention to your accomplice what you think.

7. Quit contingent upon somebody other than yourself.

Having somebody to embrace, kiss, embrace, have intercourse, and offer your life is out and out astonishing. However, before you go out into the nightfall searching for adoration, you should figure out how to cherish yourself. Similarly, as you shouldn't welcome a companion into your home when it's a muddled fiasco, you shouldn't welcome an accomplice into your life if it's not so great. Be cautious if your inside home is before welcoming another person.

Numerous terrible business choices are caused in light of the fact that pioneers to feel pushed and uncertain about their positions, their vocation ways, their own certainty, and even what others consider them.

All pioneers are feeling the squeeze and desire, from essential managers and group pioneers to CEOs and political pioneers. Subsequently, it is troublesome not to have unpleasant weaknesses and incidental sentiments of trust. All things considered, there are a lot of factors to manage. Such a huge numbers of questions that can't be considered. Such a large number of individuals question your choices. Thus, numerous characters to manage, including yours.

Obviously, we as a whole have vulnerability once in a while in light of the fact that we accept that we are sufficiently bad or that we are probably going to bomb on a specific assignment or undertaking. For pioneers, vulnerabilities can be very overpowering, particularly given the dread that disappointment may contrarily influence the association's interior economic wellbeing or future advancement.

This is the thing that frequently causes such a lot of distressing disappointment nervousness and vulnerabilities for pioneers.

The requirement for consistent approval and endorsement.

- Rumination and staying in past audits.
- Absence of trust in others, particularly in partners and bosses.

Failure to acknowledge self-flaws and botches, and a background marked by accusing missteps and blunders of outer and wild factors. Contrast yourself wrongly and the individuals who are viewed as best, both inside the association and in the business. Consolidating care into your idea designs is a solid method to oversee sentiments of instability. By concentrating consistently and every now and again right now, he starts:

Acknowledge everything about yourself without judging.

- Go past the past.

- Try not to contrast yourself as well as other people.

- Trust others more.

- Find that approving yourself is the main approval that issues.

These advantages of care were best summarized by the old Chinese savant Lao-Tse: "In light of the fact that you have confidence in yourself, you don't attempt to persuade others. Since you are happy with yourself, you needn't bother with the endorsement of others. The world acknowledges it.

How dread disturbs dynamic and how to keep it from entering

Dread has numerous approaches to infuse yourself into life and cause issues. One of the manners in which dread meddles is by occupying dynamic.

At the point when it is there, dread will, in general, carry the conduct to the most secure choice. At times moving easily is certainly the ideal approach to do it. In some cases, it can't. An excessive amount to state can meddle with numerous lives. Researchers at the University of Pittsburgh have found what happens when dread rules dynamic and convinces choices that are not the best.

Research distributed in The Journal of Neuroscience discloses how dread attempts to relax the piece of the mind that is fundamental for using sound judgment. The zone is the prefrontal cortex (PFC), at the front of the cerebrum, and is the zone that gives adaptability to dynamic.

The PFC is the piece of the mind that is engaged with gauging the outcomes, arranging, and handling musings in a sensible and levelheaded manner. It helps expel the passionate fume from a choice by quieting the amygdala, the piece of the mind that chips away at intuition, drive, and crude feelings.

The examination. What they did

The analysts watched synapse action in the PFC of restless rodents, while those rodents were urged to settle on a choice on what conduct would give them a sweet prize. Rodents have numerous organic and physiological similitude's' to people, which is the reason they are regularly utilized right now examine.

The specialists analyzed the conduct and cerebrum action of two gatherings of rodents: one that got a fake treatment and the other that got a low portion of an uneasiness causing medicine. The two gatherings of rodents had the option to use sound judgment, yet the frightful rodents committed unmistakably more errors when there was more interruption on their way.

How dread meddles. What research implies.

Nervousness uses sound judgment by lessening the cerebrum's capacity to evade interruptions. Interruptions can be physical, similar to things in nature, or they can appear as considerations and stresses. Uneasiness upsets the cerebrum's capacity to overlook this interruption by anesthetizing a gathering of neurons in the prefrontal cortex that is explicitly engaged with dynamic.

"We have adopted a shortsighted strategy to examine and to treat nervousness. We have compared it with uneasiness and have commonly expected that it over-burdens whole cerebrum circuits. In any case, this investigation shows that nervousness discharges synapses in a particular manner: Bita Moghaddam, lead creator, and Professor in the Department of Neuroscience at the University of Pittsburgh.

These new discovering difficulty customary hypotheses that attack the dread of life by over stimulating circuits in mind. It appears that with regards to deciding, uneasiness specifically breaks certain associations, making it hard for the mind to dispose of unimportant data and settle on better choices.

Step by step instructions to abstain from stressing over choices:

Fortify your mind against dread.

Be thoughtful. Care fortifies the prefrontal cortex, the piece of the cerebrum that dread can send disconnected. Without the full limit of the prefrontal cortex to impact dynamic, choices are bound to get powerful and inflexible and to be driven by meddling feelings that are not worth the impact. Care improves the mind's capacity to sift through interruptions to settle on increasingly educated and important choices. It restrains the impact of things that don't make a difference, so you can concentrate on things that do make a difference. (Kindly this article clarifies it in more detail).

Comprehend where dread truly originates from.

Work worry of ordinary worry throughout everyday life, (for example, contending or being stuck in terrible rush hour gridlock) can make enough feeling and forceful contemplations impact significant and disconnected choices. Tension can likewise emerge from past occurrences. The energy may have been legitimized at that point, however now it might disrupt the general flow. Unwarranted dread can prompt excessively sure dynamic. By seeing where dread originates from, you can lessen the impact on conduct.

Slower

Easing back down appears as though it ought to be simple; however, no, life is once in a while that simple. Easing back down includes a cognizant move from programmed contemplations and emotions to what is truly occurring, what you truly feel, and what might be behind it. A lot of our inclination and reaction to a circumstance happen naturally. In any case, it shouldn't be that way. The more we understand what we do or feel, the more force we need to transform it.

Try not to get into the possibility that contemplations, emotions, and conduct are one bundle. They are most certainly not.

Because you feel a specific way or figure, a specific idea doesn't mean you need to act a specific way. This implies we are increasingly mindful of the conduct and balance of the standard programmed response. Musings, emotions, and conduct are interrelated. They impact one another, regularly without us understanding it. Change one, and the other two will inevitably make up for a lost time. You don't need to accept this, simply check out it and perceive how it occurs.

Imagine (Yes, truly. Simply attempt it)

At the point when you have to settle on a significant choice, it is entirely expected to feel frenzy or uneasiness. However, you ought not to surge your choice. Dread is there to shield you from peril, yet on the grounds that the alert sounds doesn't mean there is a risk. Attempt to challenge the nearness and impact of dread by "imagining" that there is nothing to stress over. This may appear to be troublesome; however, the more you do it, the simpler it will be. Remain with the occasion. You are fine at the present time, and you are fine. Regardless of whether it doesn't appear to be dedicated to you, imagine it is. The fact of the matter is to lessen dread enough that you don't compel yourself to settle on choices where you don't have to.

Because there are choices that don't mean there is an inaccurate one.

What choice would you make on the off chance that you knew there is no off-base one? Frequently dread settles on dynamic, considerably progressively troublesome by causing us to accept that there will be acceptable and shrewd, a great and awful decision. In case you're truly gotten between two choices, odds are, neither one of the decisions isn't right. When you've settled on the choice, whatever it is, you'll sort out the earth around you, including your own conduct and responses, to ensure it's alright. Your perseverance, imagination, and inventiveness will increment to help you and push ahead.

Leave yourself alone guided by what you need, instead of what you need to maintain a strategic distance from.

Attempt to change your core interest. Dread will, in general, control choices by giving every one of us potential results, particularly awful ones. At that point, choices are made to stay away from what we don't need, rather than seeking what we do need. What might your choices resemble on the off chance that they were driven by what you need to occur, as opposed to what you would prefer not to occur?

Lastly

It is the type of dread pricking you from behind and afterward covering up in the shadows. Reinforcing your mind to sift through interruptions and monitoring the sentiments that drive conduct or choices will prepare for shrewdness, significance, and clearness, and for choices that will be most enhancing for you.

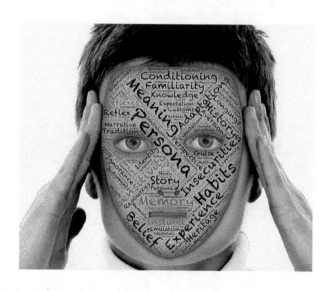

Hi, and welcome to - How to improve your confidence rapidly! I have expounded on what I believe is confidence and how I have improved mine. I am not a specialist or a specialist; however, I have pursued numerous self-improvement guides to improve my confidence, and I accept that high confidence is a significant factor in carrying on with a cheerful life.

So, what is confidence?

Your certainty can't how you feel about yourself in the present; however, how you, in a general sense, judge yourself over the long haul. On the off chance that you have low confidence, everyday occasions can bigly affect how you feel. For instance, a neighborly signal from a companion or a decent day at work can cause you to feel useful for a couple of days.

What's more, on the other hand, a not really charming day can cause you to feel very discouraged. Also, let's face it, most days are exhausting, so in the event that you have low confidence, remaining high can be a battle! Great solid confidence depends on tolerating yourself as you seem to be: know what your identity is and be fulfilled as you may be!

Your certainty is.

You were fabricated and created for a mind-blowing duration up until now! What's more, indeed, you got it, the youngsters' hood hugely affected your confidence. All the enjoyment, great, awful, and appalling things that occurred during development influenced how you rate yourself today. Sound confidence will be worked with recognition, regard, and stable impacts as you develop.

Individuals who have been loudly mishandled, routinely condemned, manhandled, don't get positive consideration, are threatened, and so on. They will experience serious difficulties in creating solid confidence.

These are outrageous models, and the unpretentious negative/positive encounters additionally have a major effect. Things you don't really recall or didn't contemplate could likewise have been significant impacts.

Examine with your 'inward voice' to help develop confidence

We, as a whole, have an internal voice that is continually prattling in our minds. Remark on all that we did/needs to do. Furthermore, it quiets and supplements individuals with sound confidence. For us with low confidence, the internal voice censures us, debilitates us, and holds us up. At the point when you accomplish something, similar to sports or a prospective employee meet-up, for instance, and somebody commends you that the internal voice says something like "he lied, you were horrible, don't trouble next time.

"What you ought to do is negate the inward voice and shoot with something like: "He lauded me for progressing admirably, it may not be great, yet win or lose, I did as well as could be expected, and I'm pleased with myself." Contending with your inward voice will improve your certainty, start now! Recall this, and YOU are in control, YOU are in charge, don't let the pundit bring you down!

Utilize positive affirmations to develop confidence.

A positive articulation is a positive proclamation about yourself. Use them in a contemplation system just as saying it to yourself consistently. In a perfect world, you need to unwind in any event once per day and smoothly rehash some positive certifications to yourself: Playing loosening up music simultaneously is great to help!

Instances of positive assertions to develop confidence:

What your identity is

- I am lovely

- I'm solid

- I'm unique

- Who will you be?

- I can be a champ

- I can be solid

- I can mend

- I can get more fit

- I will do it

- I will look, such as myself.

- I will grin more

- I'll control my state of mind.

By continually rehashing these things to yourself, you must choose the option to trust them somewhere inside! You will end up being these things, and that develops confidence.

Self-care to develop confidence

Self-training is essential to develop confidence. Start by taking physical consideration of yourself, eating great, remaining fit/getting fit, and resting as much as you need, not all that much or excessively little.

Self-training to develop confidence causes you to feel advantageous. Treat yourself consistently by doing fun and charming things, particularly in the event that you have achieved something significant. You need to compensate yourself for your accomplishments! Consider the things you like about yourself and continually remind yourself. Try not to stress over yourself or rebuff for disappointment - reward yourself for attempting first. Make sure to concentrate on the great and figure out how to pardon what you think about awful.

The minutes when you don't feel better or positive are critical, and you should discover things about yourself that are acceptable, regardless of how little! Doing these things develops confidence. Finding support from friends and family can be extraordinary assistance in developing confidence. Request that loved one's mention to you what they like about you. Request that they are out in the event that you feel discouraged or baffled: simply listening when you let off pressure can go far in developing confidence.

Your condition is essential to improve and keep up your confidence.

Being encompassed by warm and adoring individuals is a tremendous factor in confidence. Presently I realize this can't work for some; not every person has a system of loved ones. In any case, you should ensure that the ones you have in your life acknowledge you and, obviously, you should acknowledge them as they seem to be. A feeling of acknowledgment will assist you with the understanding that the contrasts between individuals are huge.

Associations with others will be assembled all the more effectively by getting this. Associate with those you see and collaborate with consistently, do this essentially by talking, contacting as you talk, demonstrating regard, tuning in, being steady, and genuine.

Adoring the individuals around you and realizing they feel a similar route about you is an extraordinary lift for your certainty!

Audit

Try not to lament what your identity is! On the off chance that and when they condemn you, for reasons unknown, you should "judge" what they are starting to you before reacting. Don't naturally apologize! In the event that the analysis is reasonable, take it with you and react with analysis. In case you are dishonest, face it, also similarly as with your inner voice. A very much formed and the self-legitimizing individual will tune in to analysis without interference and afterward react.

Make certain to scrutinize at the correct occasions; individuals with low confidence frequently think that it's harder to offer than to take. Simply let the inconvenience leave when it "bubbles," it is normally best to cut things in the bud. Be cautious and do whatever it takes not to hurt another person's confidence. Utilize "I" and not "you," for instance, I'm experiencing difficulty when that occurs.

The most effective method to turn out to be intellectually solid: procedures to manufacture versatility

A few people appear to chill out rapidly from individual mishaps and disappointments, while others think that it's considerably more troublesome. In case you are in the last grouping, don't pressure. Fortunately, there are various helpful procedures for making mental adaptability; It is a quality that can be learned and honed through preparing, discipline, and troublesome work.

Regularly, our strength is tried when living conditions become sudden and more terrible, for example, the downfall of a companion or relative, the takeoff of employment, or the completion of a relationship. In any case, such difficulties offer the chance to rise and return considerably more grounded than previously.

Peruse on to learn strategies to create and improve your psychological versatility and viably manage life's difficulties.

The most effective method to be intellectually solid

Mental quality is the capacity of a person to successfully manage stressors, weights, and challenges and to perform as well as could be expected, paying little heed to the conditions in which they get themselves (Clough, 2002).

Creating mental quality is basic to carry on with your best life. Exactly when we go to the exercise center and lift loads to build up our physical muscles, we likewise need to build up our emotional wellness using mental apparatuses and strategies. Ideal emotional well-being causes us to carry on with an actual existence we love, have significant social associations, and positive confidence. It likewise assists with facing challenges, attempts new things, and manages troublesome circumstances that life can bring us.

To be intellectually sound, we should fabricate our psychological quality! Mental quality is something that creates after some time by people who decide to focus on self-improvement.

Similarly, as we see the physical advantages of practicing and eating more advantageous, we have to create solid mental propensities, for example, rehearsing appreciation, in the event that we need to encounter emotional well-being gains.

So also, to see the physical advantages, we should likewise surrender undesirable propensities, for example, gobbling low-quality nourishment and surrender unfortunate propensities for mental increases, for example, feeling frustrated about yourself.

We are, for the most part, fit for reinforcing ourselves intellectually, and the key is to continue practicing and practicing your psychological muscles, similarly as you would on the off chance that you were attempting to build up your physical quality!

On creating flexibility and mental quality

The term 'flexibility,' which is regularly utilized corresponding to positive emotional wellness, is really taken from the system, where it alludes to the capacity of a substance or item to get once again into shape ('versatility,' 2019). Similarly, as a material article needs quality and adaptability to recoup, an individual additionally need these attributes to be intellectually safe. A comparative idea, Mental Toughness, alludes to the capacity to remain solid, notwithstanding difficulty, to keep up your concentration and assurance in spite of the troubles you experience. An intellectually troublesome individual considers them to be and the mishap as a chance, not a danger, and has the certainty and positive way to deal with taking what anticipates him (Strycharczyk, 2015).

To be intellectually safe, you have to have a specific level of obstruction, yet not every single strong individual is essentially intellectually safe. On the off chance that you think of it as a representation, the opposition would be the mountain, while mental quality could be one of the procedures to ascend that mountain.

Strycharczyk (2015) thinks that its helpful to consider the distinction as far as the expression 'endure and succeed.' Opposition causes you to endure, and mental quality encourages you to flourish.

Mental durability starts when you decide to see what is experiencing your brain, without expressly relating to those musings or emotions. At that point, discover the purpose of bringing out idealistic considerations about the circumstance.

As indicated by Strycharczyk and Clough (undated), the methods for creating mental obstruction rotate around five topics:

- Positive reasoning

- Uneasiness control

- Show

- objective

- Consideration control

Similarly, as with the improvement of mental quality, the advancement of mental quality requires mindfulness and commitment. As a rule, individuals with mental issues appear to accomplish more than they are intellectually touchy and appreciate a higher level of fulfillment.

Turner (2017) portrays four key qualities of mental quality, which he calls 4Cs: control, devotion, challenge, and certainty. One may have a portion of these properties. However, the mix of each of the four characteristics is the way to progress.

Mental sturdiness can be estimated with the MTQ48 psychometric apparatus made by Professor Peter Clough of Manchester Metropolitan University. The MTQ48 device is logically substantial and solid and depends on the 4C structure, which gauges the principle segments of mental versatility.

The 4 Cs of mental flexibility: (Turner, 2017)

1. Control

This is how much you feel in charge of your life, including your feelings and your feeling of life. The reviewing segment can be viewed as your confidence. Being high on the size of control implies that you feel great in your skin and have a decent feeling of what your identity is.

You can control your feelings, more averse to uncover your passionate state to other people, and less occupied by the feelings of others. Being low on the size of control implies that you can feel that occasions are going on to you and that you have no control or impact over what's going on.

2. Responsibility

This is the extent of your own concentration and unwavering quality. Being high on the size of duty can set objectives adequately and accomplish them reliably, without being diverted. A significant level of duty demonstrates that you are acceptable at building up schedules and propensities that advance achievement. Being low on the responsibility scale implies that you may think that it's hard to set objectives and needs, or alter schedules or propensities that show achievement. You can likewise effectively be occupied by others or by contending needs.

Together, the Control and Commitment scales speak to the flexibility part of the meaning of Mental Toughness.

This looks good considering the way that the ability to bounce from adversities requires a conclusion of understanding that you are responsible for your life and can reveal an improvement. It likewise requires focus and the capacity to set propensities and objectives that will get you in the groove again.

3. Challenge

This is how much you are driven and versatile. Satisfying the size of the text implies that you are headed to arrive at your best close to the home brand and that you see difficulties, change and misfortune as circumstances as opposed to dangers; you're presumably adaptable and nimble.

Being low on the Challenge scale implies that you can consider a change to be a danger and maintain a strategic distance from new or testing circumstances inspired by a paranoid fear of disappointment.

4. Trust

This is how much you have faith in your capacity to be beneficial and capable; It is your trust and conviction that you can impact others. To be at the highest point of the certainty scale is to accept that you will effectively finish the errands and take on mishaps while keeping up the everyday practice and, in any event, fortifying your assurance. Being low on the Confidence scale implies that difficulties effectively trouble you, and you don't think you are equipped for impacting others or have no impact on them.

Together, the Challenge and Confidence scales speak to the Confidence part of the meaning of Mental Toughness. This speaks to an individual's capacity to distinguish and take advantage of a lucky break, and view circumstances as chances to grasp and investigate. This looks good in such a case that you put stock in yourself and your aptitudes and participate viably with others, and you will undoubtedly change troubles into triumphs. The most effective method to assemble versatility in grown-ups.

As referenced before, mental flexibility can't guarantee the quality that individuals could conceivably have. It is increasingly about conduct, contemplations, and activities that everybody can learn and create. Obviously, there might be a hereditary part to an individual's degree of mental strength, yet it is absolutely something to expand on.

In an article motivated by the 2013 Society for the Study of Traumatic Stress board, Drs. Southwick, Bonanno, Masten, Panter-Brick, and Yehuda (2013) tended to probably the most squeezing ebb, and flow issues in flexibility inquire about.

Board individuals had somewhat various meanings of flexibility, yet most definitions incorporated an idea of sound, versatile, and positive working from affliction. They concurred that "versatility is a mind-boggling development and can be characterized diversely with regards to people, families, associations, social orders and societies."

There was likewise accord that the capacity to manufacture flexibility depends on numerous elements, including hereditary, formative, segment, social, financial, and social factors, notwithstanding, that versatility can be developed (Southwick et al., 2013).

Basically, versatility can be created through resolve, discipline, and difficult work; and there are numerous techniques to do this. The key is to perceive ways that are likely going to work commendably for you, like your own special segment singular adaptability improvement framework.

Increment mental quality in understudies:

Like grown-ups, intellectually solid kids and young people can handle issues, come back from disappointments, and face life's difficulties and challenges. They are versatile and have the mental fortitude and certainty of arriving at their maximum capacity.

Creating mental quality in understudies is similarly as significant, if not progressively significant, than creating mental quality in grown-ups. As indicated by Morin (2018), helping kids to create mental quality requires a triple methodology, figuring out how to:

- Supplant negative contemplations with positive, increasingly practical musings.

- Control your feelings with the goal that your feelings don't control them.

Make positive strides.

While there are numerous methodologies, discipline systems, and learning instruments that assist youngsters with building up their psychological muscles, here are ten procedures to support understudies.

1. Learn explicit abilities

Instead of committing kids languish over their errors, control ought to show kids how to improve next time. Rather than discipline, use results that show valuable abilities, for example, critical thinking and drive control.

2. Have your youngster commit errors

Missteps are an inescapable piece of life and learning. Show your kid or understudy; this is the situation and that they ought not to be embarrassed or embarrassed about having misconstrued something.

3. Show your kid how to create the sound inward exchange.

It is critical to assist kids with building up a reasonable and hopeful perspective on life and to reformulate negative considerations as they emerge. Learning this aptitude from the get-go in life will assist you with conquering troublesome occasions.

4. Urge your youngster to manage fears

Permitting a kid to confront his feelings of trepidation will assist him with increasing priceless certainty. One approach to do this is to train your youngster to escape his customary range of familiarity and face his feelings of dread bit by bit while adulating and compensating his endeavors.

5. Cause your youngster to feel awkward

It might be enticing to quiet or salvage your youngster or understudy when they are battling, yet it is imperative to allow them to lose or battle some of the time and demand that they are mindful, regardless of whether they are most certainly not. Adoring Just managing little issues can assist kids with building up their psychological quality.

6. Manufacture character

Kids with a good solid compass and worth framework will be better ready to settle on sound choices. You can help by imparting esteems like trustworthiness and empathy and consistently making learning openings that strengthen these qualities.

7. Focus on appreciation

Practicing appreciation is probably the best thing you can accomplish for your emotional wellbeing, and it's the same for kids. Appreciation encourages us to keep things in context, even in the most troublesome occasions. To bring up an intellectually solid youngster, urge him to rehearse appreciation normally.

8. Affirm moral duty

Assuming liability for your activities or missteps is likewise part of creating mental quality. In the event that your understudy attempts to censure others for the manner in which he thinks, feels, or carries on, simply send them away from the statement of regret and let them clarify.

9. Learn feeling control aptitudes

Rather than quieting or quieting your kid down at whatever point he is vexed, instruct him to manage awkward feelings freely, so he doesn't develop contingent upon you to control his state of mind. Youngsters who comprehend and experience their emotions are more ready to confront the high points and low points of life.

10. Be a good example of mental quality

What better approach to show a youngster than by model? To advance mental quality in your understudies or youngsters, you should exhibit your psychological quality.

Give them that you focus on personal growth in your life and discussion about your objectives and the means you are taking to reinforce yourself.

Different ways to manufacture and improve flexibility

As we have taken in, your degree of mental obstruction can't choose during childbirth, and it can improve all through an individual's life. Next, we will investigate various procedures and methods used to improve mental flexibility.

1. Obtaining of abilities

Procuring new aptitudes can assume a significant job in creating strength, as it builds up a feeling of dominance and capability, which can be utilized in troublesome occasions and confidence and the capacity to beat issues downloading.

The abilities to be educated rely upon the person. For instance, some may profit by improving psychological abilities, for example, working memory or specific consideration, which will help with day by day working. Others may profit by learning new pastime exercises through competency-based learning.

Procuring new aptitudes inside a gathering setting gives the additional advantage of social help, which likewise advances flexibility.

2. Objective

The capacity to create objectives, the significant strides to reach, and arrive at those objectives help create self-control and mental flexibility. Objectives can be large or little, identified with physical wellbeing, passionate prosperity, vocation, accounts, otherworldliness, or nearly anything. Focuses on that gain abilities have a twofold advantage. For instance, figuring out how to play an instrument or learning another dialect.

A few investigations demonstrate that defining and taking a shot at objectives outside of the person, that is, strict association or chipping in for a reason, can be especially useful in building strength. This can give a more profound feeling of direction and association, which can be important in troublesome occasions.

3. Controlled presentation

Controlled presentation alludes to continuous introduction to nervousness inciting circumstances and is utilized to assist individuals with beating their feelings of dread. The research proposes this can advance flexibility, particularly with regards to obtaining aptitudes and defining objectives - a triple advantage.

Open talking, for instance, is a valuable fundamental ability, yet additionally something that stirs dread in numerous individuals. Individuals who fear open talking can set objectives identified with a controlled introduction to create or obtain this particular ability. They can open themselves to a little crowd of a couple of individuals and slowly increment their crowd after some time. This kind of activity plan can be started by the individual or can be created with a specialist prepared in intellectual, social treatment. Effective endeavors can expand confidence and a feeling of independence and strength, which can all be utilized in the midst of affliction.

The American Psychological Association ('Road to Resilience,' N.D.) shares 11 systems for creating mental flexibility:

1. Make associations.

Versatility can be reinforced through our association with family, companions, and the network. Sound associations with individuals who care about you and who will tune in to your issues, bolster you in troublesome occasions, and assist us with recovering expectations. Moreover, helping other people in their period of scarcity can help us massively and advance our own feeling of versatility.

2. Maintain a strategic distance from emergencies as inconceivable issues.

We can't change the outer occasions around us, yet we can control our reaction to these occasions. Throughout everyday life, there will consistently be difficulties, yet it is essential to look past any unpleasant circumstance and recollect that conditions will change. Investigate the inconspicuous ways you can feel better when confronted with the troublesome circumstance.

3. Acknowledge that change is a piece of life.

They state that the main consistent in life is change. Because of troublesome conditions, certain objectives can never again be practical or feasible. By tolerating what you can't transform, you can concentrate on the things you control.

4. Go to your objectives. (additionally, highlighted by Whitley, 2018)

While growing long haul objectives for the 10,000-foot view is significant, ensuring they are practical is fundamental. Making little, noteworthy advances makes our objectives attainable and causes our progress in the direction of these objectives all the time, making little 'wins' en route. Attempt to step toward your objective consistently.

5. Make a definitive move.

Rather than keeping up a key good way from issues and stress and wishing they would just leave, endeavor to make an authoritative move at whatever point possible.

6. Search for open doors for self-disclosure.

Now and then, catastrophe can prompt extraordinary exercises and self-awareness. Experiencing a troublesome circumstance can expand our certainty and confidence, fortify our connections, and show us a ton about ourselves. Numerous individuals who have encountered challenges have likewise detailed more noteworthy gratefulness forever and a more profound otherworldliness.

7. Have an uplifting demeanor about yourself.

Building fearlessness can be useful in staying away from troubles and building flexibility. Having a positive perspective on yourself is urgent with regard to taking care of issues and confiding in your own sense.

8. Keep things in context.

At the point when difficulties turn crazy, consistently recollect that it tends to be more awful; attempt to abstain from blowing up things messed up. Building versatility keeps up a long-haul point of view on troublesome or agonizing occasions.

9. Look after expectation.

At the point when we center around the negative of a circumstance and stay on edge, we are more averse to discover an answer. Attempt to keep an idealistic and hopeful point of view and expect a positive outcome rather than a negative one. The representation can be a valuable procedure right now.

10. Deal with yourself.

Self-care is a fundamental technique for creating strength and helps keep the brain and body sufficiently sound to manage troublesome circumstances that emerge. Dealing with yourself implies focusing on your own needs and sentiments and taking an interest in exercises that bring you delight and unwinding. Normal exercise is, likewise, an extraordinary type of self-care.

11. Extra approaches to fabricate flexibility can be useful.

Building strength can appear changed things to changed individuals. Journaling, rehearsing appreciation, reflection, and other otherworldly practices assist some with peopling reestablish trust and reinforce their assurance.

The Path to Resilience (APA)

The American Psychological Association (2014) characterizes versatility as the way toward changing fittingly for affliction, injury, disaster, dangers, or the principle wellsprings of stress, for example, family and relationship issues, wellbeing, or work environment issues extreme and monetary stressors.

At the end of the day, "recoup" from troublesome encounters. Flexibility can't guarantee the quality that individuals might have. It incorporates practices, considerations, and activities that can be learned and created in everybody.

Research has demonstrated that flexibility is normal, normal and that individuals show strength. A genuine case of this is the response of numerous Americans to the fear-based oppressor assaults of September 11, 2001, and the endeavors of individuals to reconstruct their lives.

As per the APA, they are strong and don't imply that somebody can't troubles or misfortunes. Actually, a lot of passionate pain regularly happens in individuals who have confronted challenges and injury in their lives.

Versatility factors

Numerous variables add to the flexibility, yet considers have demonstrated that the most significant factor is having steady connections inside and outside the family. Connections that are mindful, adoring, and give consolation and consolation help develop an individual's strength.

The APA recommends a few extra factors identified with strength, including:

- The capacity to make reasonable arrangements and significant strides to execute them.

- A positive mental self-portrait and trust in your qualities and capacities.

- Correspondence and critical thinking aptitudes.

- The capacity to control and manage solid sentiments and driving forces.

- These are generally factors that individuals can create all alone.

Versatility building procedures

With regard to building versatility, procedures will fluctuate from individual to individual. We all in all respond differently to horrendous and upsetting life events, so an approach that capacities splendidly for one individual may not work for another. For example, some assortment of how to grant assumptions and how to oversee trouble may reflect social differences, etc.

Gain from quite a while ago

Taking a gander at past encounters and wellsprings of individual quality can assist you with understanding which strength advancement methodologies will work for you. The following are some significant inquiries from the American Psychological Association, which may make you wonder how you responded to testing circumstances before. By inspecting the responses to these inquiries, you can create future procedures.

- Envision the accompanying circumstance:

- What sorts of occasions have been the most distressing for me?

- How did those occasions influence me?

- Has it been useful to consider notable individuals throughout my life when I'm vexed?

- With whom have I looked for help to defeated an awful or distressing experience?

- What have I found out about myself and my associations with others in troublesome occasions?

- Has it helped me help somebody who is experiencing a comparable encounter?

- Have I had the option to beaten deterrents and, provided that this is true, how?

What gave me more trust later on?

Stay adaptable

An extreme attitude is an adaptable outlook. At the point when you experience distressing conditions and occasions throughout your life, it is useful to keep up adaptability and parity in the accompanying manners:

Permit yourself to encounter compelling feelings and acknowledge when you may need to set them aside to continue working. Step forward and find a way to confront your issues and fulfill the needs of regular day to day existence, yet additionally realize when to step back and rest/give new vitality.

Invest energy with friends and family who offer help and support; Beware.

Trust others, yet in addition, realize when to confide in yourself.

Spots to look for help

Now and then, the help of loved ones sufficiently isn't. Realize when to look for help outside of your circle. Individuals frequently think that its supportive of contacting:

Self-improvement gatherings and network support

Sharing encounters, feelings, data, and thoughts can be an extraordinary solace for individuals who can feel desolate in troublesome occasions.

Books and different productions

Tuning in to other people who have effectively explored through unfavorable circumstances, for example, the one you are experiencing, can be an extraordinary inspiration and motivation to build up an individual system.

Online assets

There is an abundance of assets and data on the Internet on the best way to manage injury and stress; ensure the data originates from a solid source.

Eminent emotional well-being is proficient

For some, the above proposals might be sufficient to manufacture versatility, however, some of the time it is perfect to search for capable help in the event that you feel that you can't work in your day by day life because of horrible accidents or other distressing occasions throughout everyday life.

Proceed with your excursion

To help condense key APA focuses, a valuable illustration for strength is to take a kayak trip. During a boating trip, you can discover a wide range of various waters: rapids, slow waters, shallow waters, and a wide range of insane bends.

Much the same as throughout everyday life, these changing conditions influence your considerations, mind-set, and the manners in which you will explore. Throughout everyday life, such as going along a waterway, it is useful to have past encounters and information. Your excursion ought to be guided by a system that most likely functions admirably for you.

Other significant angles remember certainty and conviction for your capacity to explore the occasionally rough waters and maybe with confided in allies to guide and bolster you on the excursion.

The flexibility advancement program

The Resilience Development Program for Children and Adolescents: Improving Social Competence and Self-Regulation is a creative program intended to expand strength in youngsters. The book depends on a 12-week versatility based gathering treatment program and applies subjective conduct hypothesis and methodologies. The program depicts 30 gathering meetings that work in the regions of confidence, poise, self-assurance, and adapting techniques (Karapetian Alvord, Zucker, Johnson Grados, 2011). Key abilities tended to in every meeting incorporate mindfulness, adaptable reasoning, and social fitness. Through conversation and down to earth methods, for example, pretend, bunch individuals, find out about resentment/dread administration, critical thinking, the individual feeling of the room, inward exchange, kinship abilities, and different subjects. Basics identified with social and individual prosperity. These gathering exercises help create explicit defensive components identified with strength.

The program incorporates unwinding procedures, for example, perception, quiet breathing, dynamic muscle unwinding, and yoga to develop self-guideline. To apply its exercises to the outside world, the program appoints schoolwork, network trips, and parent inclusion.

The Resilience Builder program is keen, all around considered, sequenced and organized, and offers a very much organized gathering system, solid enough for tenderfoots. In case you are scanning for an ordered program to flexibility show your child or understudy, this is an uncommon decision.

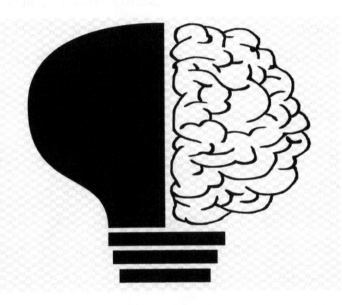

At the point when confronted with troublesome choices, it tends to be hard to realize the correct approach. Ken Costa, a long-lasting venture broker, and guide offers five stages to aid the dynamic procedure.

Settling on troublesome choices is rarely simple, regardless of what phase of life we are in. Regardless of whether we are searching for that initial step on the profession stepping stool or we as of now have work and are presently thinking about another scale, it tends to be hard to realize the correct way to take. Be that as it may, there are steps we can take in the event that we need to use sound judgment.

It's typical for individuals to move to and from between various alternatives, regardless of whether it's a vocation, cash, business, opportunity, or even relationship-related. How would you realize which is the best alternative for you in a given circumstance? Here and there, it is anything but difficult to settle on the correct choices. However, some of the time, various choices appear to be the best alternative. A considerable lot of them likewise appear to prompt laments or botched chances.

Fortunately, settling on cool-headed choices involves gauging the potential upsides and downsides of each accessible result. The following is a basic three-advance procedure to assist you with settling on cool-headed choices regardless of what part of your life they may influence.

1) What are the prizes?

In the event that you can browse more than one alternative, an astounding first inquiry for every one of them is: "The thing that does picking this choice offer me?" If the prizes are enormous, you might be happy to endure some danger of exploiting the result. Alternately, if the payout is little, you may not have a sense of security to chance, particularly if the dangers are great.

2) What are the weaknesses?

At that point, consider what you can lose if the choice doesn't work. While positive reasoning is acceptable, looking forward and pondering potential disadvantages can spare a great deal of agony. On the off chance that your misfortunes can be tremendous with a specific choice, you may choose to hold up some time to check whether the changes improve after some time. On the off chance that there are downsides, yet the dangers are little, the choice appears to be all the more encouraging.

3) What is the most terrible that can occur?

At last, go above and beyond and ask, "What is the most exceedingly terrible thing that can occur on the off chance that I pick this alternative, and would I acknowledge those results?" It might appear to be a skeptical inquiry; however, explaining the circumstance is incredibly powerful! On the off chance that you can't deal with the results of such a choice, you quickly realize that it can't make the most reasonable choice for you at the present time. Notwithstanding, on the off chance that you can deal with the outcomes, positive or negative, this is a practical choice for you.

Frequently all choices offer moderately equivalent prizes and disadvantages, and settling on brilliant choices is troublesome! It is constantly essential to tune in to your senses. What does that little voice say to you in the rear of your head? Regularly this is substantially more exact than any thinking. However, we attempt to ace it with rationale. Simply hear it out!

With regard to that, there is no settled method to settle on an astute choice. Simply gauge the upsides and downsides, tune in to your instinct, and put forth a valiant effort. "Wrong" choices can regularly open up a totally different chance or circumstance that we hadn't considered, and end up being the best! Remember to gain from all circumstances, and furthermore, that creates a choice is obviously superior to putting off. As you settle on more choices, your certainty will develop, and settling on savvy choices will get simpler and simpler.

The most effective method to settle on keen choices at home, grinding away, and anyplace. In life, we face numerous choices. Do you realize that the normal individual settles on a huge number of choices consistently?

These range from the schedule that is redundant and frequently conflicting to significant choices that have enduring ramifications for our lives and those of others.

Huge numbers of the significant choices we should make in life require cautious thought and thought of numerous issues, so accepting a word of wisdom can be exceptionally useful. Learning the correct choices frequently needs the support of everyone around us. Nearly everybody gets counsel from somebody. Individuals rely upon companions, partners, guardians, kin, advisors, ministers, coaches, and numerous others for counsel or dynamic help.

Getting a word of wisdom is a workmanship that can be sharpened through training. It doesn't easily fall into place, yet you can learn it cautiously. There are those whose lives have been enhanced by the nature of the choices they have caused dependent on a word of wisdom; they too, have gotten from others.

In this manner, the nature of our lives is impacted by the individuals from whom we get counsel. For every one of us, there are individuals who enhance our lives and other people who channel our lives because of the nature of the guidance they give us.

So as to push ahead throughout everyday life, to truly figure out how to settle on trustworthy choices, at home, grinding away, and all over the place, you should inquire about and decide the nature of the individuals you get counsel from to give consistent consideration rather than inappropriate guidance.

Regardless of whether you get great and flawed guidance on a specific issue, it should be conceivable to comprehend what to search for. That capacity to recognize great and awful guidance is one of the most significant strides in getting solid counsel and settling on quality choices that assist you with pushing ahead in your life.

Approaches to settle on better choices

To use sound judgment, we have to adjust the apparently inverse powers of feeling and discernment. We should have the option to foresee the future, watch the present circumstance precisely, comprehend the psyches of others, and face vulnerability.

The greater part of us disregard the psychological procedures behind our choices, yet this has become a hotly debated issue for a look into, and luckily what clinicians and neurobiologists find can assist us with settling on better choices. Here, we unite a portion of his many interesting revelations in the New Scientist's Guide to settle on a choice.

1 Don't fear the outcomes

Regardless of whether it's a long end of the week in Paris or an outing to the ski slants, another vehicle or a greater house, or even who to wed, pretty much every choice we make includes foreseeing what's to come. Regardless, we envision how the aftereffects of our decisions will cause us to feel and what the enthusiastic or "decadent" results of our activities will be. Carefully, we, by and large, pick the alternative that we accept will make us most joyful, generally speaking.

These 'full of feeling conjectures' are fine in principle. Individuals routinely overestimate the effect of choice results and life occasions, both great and terrible. We will, in general, imagine that triumphant the lottery will make us more joyful than it truly will be, and life would be totally deplorable on the off chance that we lost the utilization of our legs. "The libertine results of most occasions are less exceptional and shorter than a great many people think," says clinician Daniel Gilbert of Harvard University. This applies to unimportant occasions like heading off to a major café just as large ones like losing an employment or a kidney.

A significant factor that drives us to make terrible forecasts is "misfortune repugnance," the conviction that misfortune will sting more than the comparing gain. For instance, Princeton University analyst Daniel Kahneman found that a great many people would prefer not to acknowledge a 50:50 wager except if the sum they can win is generally twofold the sum they could lose.

Hence, a great many people would possibly wager £ 5 with a coin flip in the event that they could win more than £ 10. All things considered, Gilbert and partners as of late demonstrated that while misfortune repugnance influenced individuals' decisions, it was substantially less excruciating than they anticipated (Psychological Science, vol 17, p 649). He ascribes this to our unrecognized mental opposition and our capacity to legitimize practically any circumstance. "We are truly adept at discovering it

So, what should a poor full of feeling indicator do? As opposed to looking and envisioning how a specific result may cause you to feel, attempt to discover somebody who settles on a similar decision or alternative, and perceive how it felt. Additionally, recall that paying little heed to what's in store, you are probably going to do less or be less satisfied than you can envision. All things considered, don't generally play safe. The most exceedingly awful may never occur, and on the off chance that it happens, you have the mental versatility in managing it.

2 Go with your nature

It's enticing to feel that creating great choices sets aside effort to methodically gauge all the upsides and downsides of various other options, yet at times a snappy preliminary or instinctual decision is similarly as acceptable, if worse.

In our day by day lives, we settle on snappy and skillful choices about who to trust and with whom we associate. Janine Willis and Alexander Todorov of Princeton University found that inside the initial 100 milliseconds of seeing another face, we judge somebody's dependability, ability, forcefulness, compassion, and engaging quality.

Think about your feelings

You may believe that feelings are the foe of dynamic, yet in reality, they are a basic piece of it. Our most fundamental feelings have developed to permit us to settle on brisk and oblivious choices in circumstances that compromise our endurance. Dread prompts flight or battle; disturb prompts evasion. Not with standing, the job of feelings in dynamic goes a lot further than these hard reactions. Each time you settle on a choice, your limbic framework, the enthusiastic focal point of the cerebrum, is dynamic.

Feelings are plainly a basic piece of the neurobiology of decision, yet whether they generally permit us to settle on the correct choices is another issue.

In case you endeavor to choose decisions influenced by an inclination, this can genuinely impact the result.

Take outrage. Daniel Fessler and partners at the University of California, Los Angeles, irritated a gathering of subjects by having them compose a paper about an encounter that turned them red.

At that point, they were permitted to play a game wherein they were given a basic choice: either an ensured installment of $ 15, or wager on additional with the possibility of winning nothing.

The analysts found that men, yet not ladies, played more when they were furious.

Diminishes on edge connections

Connection hypothesis became out of crafted by John Bowlby, who was the principal therapist to introduce the thought behind a lot of current psychotherapy: that a youngster's closeness and feeling that all is well with the world with their essential parental figure assume a basic job. How protected that kid will be as a grown-up. After some time, clinicians have additionally refined this plan to guarantee that youth connection designs anticipate grown-up connection styles in sentimental connections in grown-up life.

While the specific wording may fluctuate contingent upon the master being counseled, for grown-up connection styles, there are commonly four flavors:

Sure: "Being close is simple!"

Tensely concerned: "I need to be sincerely private with individuals, yet they would prefer not to be with me!"

Scornful avoider: "I'd preferably not rely upon others or let others rely upon me!"

Restlessly maintaining a strategic distance from: "I need to be near, however, consider the possibility that I get injured.

Evasion and dread related to expanded weakness of connection are, without a doubt, the principle gives that a considerable lot of us battle within treatment consistently and once in a while a seemingly endless amount of time after year.

Get over

I am, or if nothing else was a course reading or maybe even extraordinary, an instance of dread and evasion. For quite a long time, I was so deadened by the dread of close connections that I had nothing with a companion until I was 28 years of age. And still, after all that, an additional eight years went before they had a long and genuine relationship, similarly as they needed.

There are numerous things that clarify this juvenile development (melancholy, injury, and numerous anxieties, also the tenacity and strange pride). However, the entirety of that clarifies how I got over it and in the long run, turned into a spouse and mother (and the writer of a book total about catastrophe) was the persistence and care of a genuinely skilled advisor, that and the medications that treated my downturn and social tension. Also, in spite of the fact that I realize I have far to go, closeness is as yet a battle for me, as those near me will affirm, I just know my style of connection, and the advancement I have made so far reinforces me for all the work I need to do.

But on the other hand, it's unimaginably consoling to me that similarly as it was a typical example for on edge and sly individuals when it went to my personal connections, I'm currently a common example for somebody who sort of got over it. Research on connection hypothesis focuses an energizing way: Just on the grounds that a grown-up as a grown-up experiences connection issues that contrarily influence their sentimental connections; it doesn't mean they will be until the end of time.

Five different ways to defeat relationship insecurity

In the event that you think you are shakily joined, and it negatively affects your adoration life, here are some sound advances you can take to make progress to make sure about connection:

Gain proficiency with your connection design by perusing the connection hypothesis. I couldn't care less if it's through Wikipedia, a scholastic article like "Connection Bonds in Romantic Relationships" or inundation in a book like Attachment, by Amir Levin and Rachel S.F. Heller, therapist and neuroscientist, individually. Trust me: information is power.

If you don't start at now have an uncommon master with association speculation, find one. It may even legitimacy inquisitive with regards to whether they have ever had a patient or client that they have seen jump from inconsistent association with ensuring around one in their wistful adult associations.

Find associates with secure association styles. The specific inverse thing you need when endeavoring to review your association style is to be undermined by someone who can't reinforce you. Research shows that around 50 percent of adults are secure in their association style, an incredible opportunity to find someone who will change their existence AND be ensured. Studies recommend that a helpful inclusion in a securely strengthened individual may, at last, cover their uncertain main impetuses.

In case you haven't found an assistant like that, go to Couples Therapy. For instance, in the event that you are on edge and are as of now having an unsanctioned romance with somebody you are on edge about, for instance, staying away from, I would suggest finding a relationship advisor who can help you both be progressively secure together. Regardless of whether you have an inclination that your relationship is working out in a good way, consider making this stride as a pre-emptive assault on issues.

Practice Isn't discussing kisses your thing? Ensure you do this regardless of whether you should begin conversing with a squishy toy. Do you detest discussing the fate of your relationship? On the off chance that you can't talk for quite a long time to come, take a stab at discussing the following hardly any months of your relationship.

It is in like manner basic to observe that sheltered holding in close associations does not simply make those associations all the more satisfying; There are signs that you may relate even with those with whom you are not wealthier.

Research demonstrates that developing self-security here and there ('security of security' in mental circles), for the most part, makes individuals progressively liberal and caring. This examination by driving connection analysts shows that "the sentiment of connection security, regardless of whether installed in an individual's long-haul relationship history or driven by subliminal or supra criminal preparation, increments philanthropic concern."

I think for those attempting to improve their riding style from hazardous to make sure about, as the maxim goes, it resembles accelerating: when you have it, you have it. After some time, you can even now provoke yourself to turn into a "superior rider," a more grounded, quicker, and progressively lithe one; however, once you look forward and ace accelerating simultaneously, you're all set to go on edge connection style signs and how it harms your connections. Our connection style impacts everything from our decision of accomplice to our conduct, seeing someone.

The restless connection style is only a connection style, yet investigates recommend it is especially harming. Prior to proceeding, let us quickly outline the connection hypothesis. Therapist John Bowlby begat the term Attachment Theory and utilized it to clarify that kids must bond with an essential parental figure. In the event that this parental figure doesn't react enticingly, we structure specific kinds of connections. The edge connection style is one of these connection styles.

There are four styles of connections:

1. Secure affirmation

The essential parental figure is completely receptive to the kid's needs and reacts likewise and on schedule. The youngster has a sense of safety enough to utilize the grown-up as a protected base to investigate his condition.

2. Connections to stay away from

On account of the avoidant connection, the essential parental figure can't accessible and can't to the kid's need. They don't react when the child is vexed—the youngster figures out how to quiet down and deal with himself.

3. Undecided/Anxious Attachment

This parental figure can't with his reactions. Now and again, they feed, and once in a while, they are insensitive. Along these lines, the kid becomes befuddled, not recognizing what response he will have. They need their folks' consideration, but since they are so erratic, they don't confide in them.

4. Scattered connection

This is the most exceedingly terrible kind of connection and happens when an infant is manhandled by its parental figure. The kid critically needs love and warmth. However, the individual who needs it is his abuser. In these cases, the kid, for the most part, separates himself from himself to endure. Since youngsters' structure, certain connection styles do as well, grown-ups.

Affirmation styles in grown-ups:

Protection

Grown-ups with a safe connection style are alright with closeness. They won't stress over dismissal and will be as glad relying upon their accomplice as their accomplice will rely upon them.

Avoidant

This individual will feel awkward when their accomplice gets excessively close. They don't care for protection, they don't need their accomplice to rely upon them, and they will value their opportunity.

Restless

Individuals with a restless connection will long for closeness and closeness. They need to draw nearer to their accomplices and, by and large, feel shaky about their relationship.

On edge and equivocal

This individual has closeness issues, yet is worried about their accomplice's promise to them. They think that it's hard to draw near to others since they dread they will be harmed on the off chance that they do.

What are the indications of the on-edge connection style?

Grown-ups with a dreadful connection style by and large view their lives adversely. They experience progressively negative feelings, think increasingly negative considerations, and respond all the more contrarily. This, obviously, affects your connections.

They will, in general, overlook positive encounters, yet center on what turned out badly in their lives. This hue is present in each part of your life. Subsequently, they are bound to encounter gloom, lower confidence, less fearlessness, and fewer fulfillments with life.

So, what are the indications of an on-edge connection style with regards to connections?

- You need consistent verification that you are adored.

- You feel shaky inside the relationship.

- He is constantly worried that they will be dismissed.

- She was continually occupied with the relationship.

- You figure your accomplice will surrender you.

- Show tender practices like consistent PDAs.

- Extremely destitute and infantile in their sentiments.

- You have extremely terrible individual cutoff points.

- Contribute a lot of vitality obsessing about what the other individual needs.

- I can't comprehend why your accomplice may require individual space.

- It generally raises family issues of dismissal.

- Grumpy and insane, enthusiastic, regularly tempests, and fits of rage.

- Dislike the scarcest and make a huge deal about it.

- It joins the accomplice's conduct too by and by.

- Correspondence through debates or clashes will energize your accomplice.

- Continuously accuse others, don't be mindful.

If they don't get the worship they need, they will undoubtedly undermine their assistant. They will rapidly change from becoming hopelessly enamored to longing for freedom. How does an on-edge connection style hurt your relationship?

Those with a frightful connection style are adoring and continually care about their accomplice. They need to go through 24 hours per day with their accomplice. It won't be exceptional for them to regulate their accomplices. They stress over dismissal, become desirous of potential adversaries, and put forth a valiant effort to satisfy their accomplice.

His principal concern is relinquishment through misdirection. Subsequently, they are consistently watching out for indications of disloyalty.

At the point when an individual with a restless connection style sees an indication of dismissal, they change their conduct to spare the relationship. This is designated "accomplice maintenance conduct" and shifts by sexual orientation.

Male accomplice maintenance incorporates:

- Clear resources

- Consistent consistency

- Rebuffing an accomplice's disloyalty

- Restraining infrastructure time

- Create desire

- Passionate control and responsibility.

- Strayed estimations

- Savagery against rivals

- Accommodation and mortification

- The maintenance conduct of ladies incorporates:

- Improving appearance

- Overstated articulations of friendship

- Overstated sexual conduct

- Caring conduct

Instructions to conquer on edge connection issues seeing someone comprehend that your accomplice may have an alternate connection to yours. This style of connection is said to have begun in youth and has nothing to do with their relationship.

Individuals with a high and frightful connection style need steady solace and love.

They esteem your accomplice's trust and duty. Finally, it is a savvy thought for the couple with a nervous association style to work on their certainty and assurance. They should make sense of how to be dynamically free. In case they can't do it without anybody's assistance, they may consider treatment to assist take with the minding of youth issues.

- Comprehend unreliable restless connections

- Comprehend restless connections

People are brought into the world with a solid endurance impulse. One of the most grounded depends on a youngster's powerlessness to endure autonomously and his total reliance on a grown-up for his consideration and assurance. Infants have an intrinsic drive to guarantee that their folks, guardians, or other notable individual meets their fundamental needs throughout everyday life. Various youngsters create various systems to achieve this, contingent upon the enthusiastic condition and the sort of care accessible to them. Connection hypothesis is the investigation of this crude sense, and specialists have isolated the different methodologies into four classifications of connection designs: secure connection and two kinds of uncertain connection, avoidant connection, and dreadful connection. The fourth class of connection, known as a complicated connection, happens when a composed procedure can't.

Connection agents have distinguished compromise as huge in shaping a connection. Tuning implies being incongruity; be mindful and react to another. Enthusiastic attunement implies that you are the first incongruity with yourself, at that point with another, lastly, with conditions. Attunement and connection are identified with the way that a grown-up, accessible, tuned, and responsive to the requirements of a kid, from adolescence, builds up a safe connection for that kid. This arrangement makes a strong establishment from which that kid can investigate the world.

The absence of attunement or misalignment of a parent or essential guardian brings about a shaky connection that creates in the relationship with their youngster. In another article, I examine how a hesitant connection design creates when guardians are cool, relationally stunted, and far off, and kids at that point attempt to close down their consciousness of their essential needs. This article will clarify how a conflicted/restless connection creates in youth and influences individuals in their grown-up connections.

What is irresolute/on edge connection?

Numerous guardians and/or parental figures are not continually in line with their kids. Connection scientists portray the conduct of these grown-ups and see how they here and there support, tune in, and react viably to their youngsters' trouble, while different occasions they are forceful, hard, or relationally repressed.

At the point when guardians flounder between these two altogether different responses, their youngsters become befuddled and shaky, not comprehending what sort of treatment to anticipate. These youngsters frequently feel suspicious or suspicious of their folks, yet are adoring and edgy.

They discover that the ideal approach to address their issues is to adhere to their connection figure. These youngsters have an undecided/on edge bond with their capricious guardians.

What conduct is related to an on-edge connection design?

Youngsters with an irresolute/on edge connection design will, in general, stick to their connection figures and frequently act frantically for their consideration. Mary Ainsworth, who evaluated the connection examples of kids ages 12 to year and a half, noticed that when youngsters with restless connections were brought together with their moms, they were confounded, shocked, or energized; investigate space and keep away from the direct eye to eye connection with it.

All things considered, these youngsters, by and large, clung to the mother. They remained strongly centered around their mom; however, they didn't appear to be glad or ameliorated. The concentration and constrained reactions of these kids forestalled further games or exploratory practices.

How does an on-edge connection design create in kids?

A few elements can add to the development of a dreadful connection design among guardians and youngsters. The most significant factor in building up an irresolute/restless connection design in a kid is conflicting attunement in the relationship with their essential guardian.

Studies have indicated that the nature of the child-rearing relationship assumes a focal job in transmitting explicit connection designs starting with one age then onto the next. Accordingly, a youngster imitates his folks' irresolute/on edge connection methodologies. Moreover, inquire about has additionally demonstrated that guardians' parental practices will, in the general mirror, the particular connection design they created as youngsters with their folks.

Hence, guardians who have grown up with a restless connection are conflicting in the manner they cooperate with their kids, to which their kids react by shaping their own on edge connection designs. A large number of these guardians and parental figures experience incredible sentiments of passionate want their youngsters because of the problematic and conflicting parenthood they have encountered.

They act hard and forceful when they mistake enthusiastic yearn for certified love for their kid.

In Compassionate Child-Crianza, Robert Firestone depicts how guardians confound their sentiments of want and the craving to get their youngster's affection with genuine love and worry for the kid's prosperity. These guardians might be overprotective or attempt to live by implication through their kid, or spotlight on their kid's appearance and execution.

They frequently cross their youngsters' very own limits by over-contacting them and disregarding their security.

How does an on-edge connection show itself in adulthood?

Youngsters who have a restless connection frequently grow up with concerned connection designs. As grown-ups, they are frequently self-basic and shaky. They look for the endorsement and consolation of others, yet this never reduces their questions. In their connections, profound emotions that they will be dismissed make them stress and not trust them. This leads them to carry on affectionately and feels excessively subject to their accomplice. These individuals' lives are not adjusted: their instability betrays them and makes them genuinely urgent in their connections.

Grown-ups with concerned connection designs regularly feel sad and assume the job of the 'persecutor' in a relationship.

They frequently have an uplifting point of view toward others, particularly their folks and their accomplice, and for the most part, have a negative attitude toward themselves.

They depend vigorously on their accomplice to approve their confidence. Since they grew up shaky because of the conflicting accessibility of their parental figures, they are 'touchy to dismissal.' They envision dismissal or deserting and search for signs that their accomplice is losing interest.

These individuals are regularly headed to actualize preventive techniques to abstain from being dismissed. Be that as it may, their unnecessary reliance, requests, and possessiveness will in general reverse discharge and quicken the give up they dread. Connection scholars and specialists Shaver and Clark (1994) have noticed that "concerned" accomplices have all the earmarks of being "continually careful and fairly dramatic." They feel furious and upset when their accomplice doesn't give them the consideration and quiet, they need.

They regularly accept that the other individual is probably not going to react to them except if they drastically express their dread and outrage. Huge numbers of those with concerned connections are hesitant to communicate their irate sentiments toward an accomplice because of a paranoid fear of conceivable misfortune or dismissal. At the point when they attempt to smother their displeasure, their conduct will, in general, waver between upheavals of outrage and supplications for pardoning and backing. At times, fears and tensions can prompt progressively genuine, enthusiastic issues, for example, sorrow.

How do connection designs bolster the basic, inward voice?

Skeptical convictions and desires related to grown-up's connection designs are strengthened by ruinous musings or basic, inward voices about themselves, others, and the world on the loose. These basic voices emphatically impact somebody's relationship style in a close connection.

Individuals with concerned grown-up connections have 'voices' that help their conviction that the world is a sincerely untrustworthy spot, brimming with uncertainty and the conceivable loss of friends and family. Instances of your voice assaults include: "Unmistakably, he/she is losing enthusiasm for you." "For what reason isn't he/she all the more adoring?" "He/she generally has a reason for not having any desire to have intercourse."

"You are so destitute and subordinate. No big surprise. They don't care for you. "He/she doesn't adore you as much as you love him".

In what capacity can an individual transform an on-edge connection into a protected connection?

Luckily, an individual's connection style can be looked into through new encounters, through collaboration with a band together with a past filled with a secure connection, and through psychotherapy. Another powerful method to build up a safe connection in adulthood is to comprehend its history. As indicated by Dr. Dan Siegel, inquire about on connection shows that "the best indicator of a kid's connection security can't occur to his folks as kids, however how his folks comprehended those youth encounters."

The way to "comprehending" somebody's beneficial encounters is to compose a rational story that encourages them to see how their youth encounters despite everything influence them today in the Psych Alive online course with Drs. Dan Siegel and Lisa Firestone will direct individuals through the way toward making a sound story to assist them with building more beneficial and more secure connections and fortify their very own feeling of enthusiastic obstruction. On the off chance that somebody makes a lucid story, the interface thinks carefully to develop fearlessness and connections progressively.

In the couple's treatment, the two gatherings can experience the voice treatment process, which will assist them with recognizing and challenge basic internal voices that advance desires for dismissal and fuel their sentiments of outrage. In their meetings, individuals can "part with," that is, uncover their self-analysis and their antagonistic and critical disposition to the next.

All in all, in viable relationship treatment, the two accomplices uncover and challenge their basic, inward voices and start to comprehend the wellspring of their damaging contemplations and perspectives with regards to their initial connections.

This methodology makes way for investigating new and progressively constructive methods for joining forces, liberating individuals to encounter authentic sentiments of adoration, and certifiable security in their close connections.

Manufacture trust

Fearlessness originates from inside. In any case, a few spots referenced that you assemble trust without it. Models are learning ability, accomplishing an objective, dressing properly, or changing your physical appearance. You will surely improve your certainty with these techniques. However, it won't be the reason for your absence of certainty.

Since fearlessness originates from inside, you should enter to get to it. Most books request that you look outside to build your certainty. Rioting to pick up certainty can make avoid. A gap that you can't find what's going on inside you. You won't have the option to distinguish the reasons for your absence of certainty. Right now, certainty can't depend on a strong establishment.

Genuine trust originates from confidence and outlook. You can be capable in certain regions, yet you don't have certainty. Then again, have you met somebody who can't awesome in any region, however, who is certain? This shows certainty may have nothing to do with execution, aptitudes, or appearance. The main thing is your convictions about yourself.

Disappointment can't

Something different, look at disillusionment. It is protected to state that you are crippled when you are hit by disillusionment? Do you despair when things don't go your course? We, all in all, do escape from the conviction that "disappointment is a disappointment." We figured out how to accept that disappointment is disappointment at school. Consider the test outcome we were reluctant to get. It has influenced our trust in ourselves today.

Disappointment can't. Disappointment is just input that something can't. With this new conviction, there will be no more disappointments throughout your life, and there might be remarks and exercises. All things considered; nothing will stop you; you can fly like a hawk. By changing just, a single conviction, you manufacture trust.

Experience life

Grasp the mentality of encountering life. Life should be loaded with experience. With this attitude, you will see and do things any other way. When you begin to accept that you are here to encounter life, you will pick up certainty and mental fortitude to do things you have never done or things you generally dread.

Beginning a discussion with an outsider turns out to be simple when you believe it's tied in with having a discussion with someone else, another experience. Notwithstanding a decent discussion or an acrid discussion, it is another experience for you.

So, the final product never again matters. Since it is tied in with encountering life. By building experience, you increment fearlessness. You will find that self-assurance manufactures self-assurance. In any case, first, you access the fearlessness that is as of now inside you. To do this, change from results-arranged to encounter situated.

Kill the view of others.

More often than not, the absence of certainty originates from the dread of how others see you. Kill this dread, and it will build your certainty for a significant distance.

The explanation we don't do the things we need to do is by and large since we dread the impression of others. A few people are reluctant to sing so anyone can hear in light of the fact that they fear how others will feel about them. I was one of them.

The day I chose to remove this dread and sing it how I need, I understood that no one cares how I sing. The individuals who thought about him are odd, so it doesn't make a difference at any rate.

How others see you is their experience; it has nothing to do with you. His understanding can't tell the truth. On the off chance that others think you sing gravely, that is their experience. You are just yourself. You don't need to purchase their story.

Your certainty will prosper when you choose to put stock in yourself than in as far as others can tell.

My goal here is to give you certainty from the back to front. Self-assurance has consistently been in you, and it is consistently there. As opposed to stating you have to fabricate your trust, it ought to be even more a rediscovery of your trust. Change your convictions without help, practice the three different ways referenced previously.

Perceive how your certainty increments. Lee Joe is an inspirational conduct mentor, coach, and speaker who has been preparing since

2003 and has motivated in excess of 10,000 lives up until this point. He prepares in modules like group building, introduction aptitudes, and mental change.

Why creating self-assurance is additionally significant for confidence. Self-assurance is an internal feeling of total security for yourself and your own capacities.

Effective individuals realize that that generally will be fruitful, we should initially believe in our own capacities. It begins with our brain, and this inclination is anticipated into our psyche.

It is simply the condition of accepting; what we bring to the table and what we can accomplish.

It's a well-known fact, in this manner, that self-assurance is critical to make progress in any aspect of our lives.

Be that as it may, what is self-assurance?

It is just a perspective. The outlook will shape our mentality, and this demeanor can be educated. By figuring out how to develop these perspectives intentionally, we can figure out how to have self-assurance.

The feeling of self-assurance is additionally identified with our confidence.

You see yourself as is our very own individual appraisal worth and worth as an individual, for yourself compared to other people. Without a sensible level of confidence, it is difficult to show a feeling of self-assurance.

Having an elevated level of confidence is a significant factor in creating solid self-assurance and the other way around. By figuring out how to be sure and improve the worth we place on ourselves, we can incredibly improve our lives.

Our way of figuring out how to believe our own capacities incorporates fortitude. Mental fortitude will assist us in building our certainty since it has to do with confronting our dread.

Normally, the absence of certainty is brought about by the mind-boggling sentiment of dread, particularly dread of the obscure. These apprehensions are firmly identified with execution uneasiness, deride, dismissal, lack of respect, and inclinations that are commonly unwarranted once occasions end.

Our capacity to work appropriately and successfully will be undermined and frustrated if these unreasonable feelings of dread are not stood up to and survived. We, as a whole, have certainty. Our certainty can vary all over. This inclination is reflected in various territories and times of our life.

It relies upon day by day challenges and on our own capacity to address those difficulties. Our certainty might be communicated in certain zones, yet it might be deficient in others.

Nonetheless, our feeling of self-assurance and high confidence can be viewed as pomposity on our part. Haughty individuals appear to be sheltered and sure.

In all actuality, haughty individuals don't generally have certainty. They go through pomposity to make for their absence of certainty.

In the event that we are certain, we will be sufficiently modest to acknowledge that we are not in every case, right. We will be willing and prepared to think about others' conclusions and won't be furious if our thoughts and suppositions are addressed.

Certain individuals acknowledge invigorating conversations and, for the most part, concur that they oppose this idea. We should make progress toward a reasonable and solid feeling of self-assurance.

Adjusted and maintainable fearlessness can be accomplished.

The expansion in our certainty must be the aftereffect of our all-around considered activity plan. It is basic to comprehend from the earliest starting point that the explanation we don't have faith in our own capacity is on the grounds that we settle on the cognizant choice not to.

I rehash, it is the self-attestation of our own failure, by not accepting that we can do it right! We should stay away from this enthusiastic snare from the earliest starting point; in light of the fact that as we accept, we will do it!

This simple, however, the tremendously sincerely fulfilling act will fortify our brains and assist us with picking up certainty. As we practice what we put stock in and assemble our certainty, we will make more triumphs in our lives.

These triumphs will fortify the development of our certainty. When our fearlessness is driven by the constructive outcomes and triumphs that we ceaselessly appreciate, our confidence; Our own worth will likewise increment!

Figuring out how to assemble trust is a procedure. The individuals who need to pay attention to their self-assurance are not hampered by difficulties, yet roused by them. Much the same as building up our muscles, we build up our self-assurance in an efficient and decided manner. With each little accomplishment, we will increase some improved certainty.

- Every accomplishment adds to creating fearlessness.

- Hit the nail on the head, begin building trust

- So how would you plan to fabricate trust?

Absence of trust? You should first completely perceive and comprehend the issue and find a way to discover an answer.

At that point, you need to begin instructing yourself. This is the progression it will take until the end of time. We should constantly learn to gain genuine ground.

Something critical to comprehend is that building trust is a procedure. It won't occur without any forethought, yet you can begin to see and feel the outcomes when you begin working reliably. Fortunately, assembling trust is something that can be effortlessly cultivated with little information and continued exertion.

As you practice what you realize and manufacture certainty, you will likewise make more accomplishments throughout your life. These triumphs will reinforce the development of your self-assurance. The outcome is a snowball impact that causes you to learn more securely than anticipated.

Trust constructs trust! Regardless of whether your self-assurance is more than once exhibited by the positive outcomes you find in your life, your questions will vanish in ancient history and vanish for all time.

The idea approach to move toward trust building is to experience the procedure bit by bit, and the initial step to any significant exertion ought to consistently be to be readied.

Plan

To plan, you should obviously distinguish where you are and where you need to be. At precisely that point, would you have the option to make a ground-breaking course of action to show up? You know where you remain as far as fearlessness.

You know the kinds of circumstances that you can serenely deal with and the sorts of circumstances that you experience issues with. Consider this for a minute and attempt to get away from where you are presently on your way to trust.

Presently consider where you might want to be. Pictures are a ground-breaking mental apparatus. Envision yourself doing the things that right now cause you to feel awkward. At the point when you do this, envision doing these things easily, totally loose inside, as though it was something you had aced and finished multiple times. On the off chance that your brain can think it, it can do it. Presently you have an away from where you are and something you need to accomplish. Ward these psychological pictures off or record them, this is your inspiration, and you can come back to them when important.

Do your brain right.

The following stage to get ready is to have the correct mentality. You should accept that your objectives are conceivable before you can sensibly focus on them.

On the off chance that this is hard for you, remember to think intelligibly and reasonably. In the event that you consider this objective reason, it becomes clearer that in addition to the fact that it is conceivable, you can likely accomplish it.

Throughout the years, a huge number of individuals have attempted, tried, and demonstrated these self-assurance building rehearses for you and me. Humankind has had sufficient opportunity and experiments to find what works and what doesn't. Have confidence that the data is there and that what you need is extremely conceivable.

Presently take out any uncertainty about it. Acknowledge it soundly and proceed onward.

Quit hitting you

Another significant piece of your belief is to quit neutralizing yourself. We will, in general, get unfortunate propensities that convey antagonism in our psyches. Put forth a cognizant attempt to dispose of pointless considerations and quit saying something that discourages you. They don't call these unfortunate propensities "pointless" to no end. That is actually what they do! You have frequently heard "think constructive" and will keep on hearing it when you ask individuals who realize how to trust. Remain positive, remain centered, and make a move.

Inspect your qualities and assess them objectively

The ideal approach to perceive your qualities is to require some serious energy and consider it your whole life. Start when you need to discover recollections of each significant accomplishment in your life. Notwithstanding what your identity is, I guarantee you there will be many. Try not to limit. If you like it, it's significant. Expound on it If you won a second-rate class foot race and recollect the extraordinary inclination you had from that point forward, include it. Do you have crafted by five interviewees? Include it. Aggregate a rundown. This is something you frequently allude to (in any event once every week) to advise you that you are very equipped for succeeding. Concentrate and feature the ones that are generally imperative to you.

Examine your rundown

Presently take a gander at the rundown and think as far as the things you are OK with the present moment and the things that, despite everything, make you awkward. Would you be able to see the patterns? You should begin to see where your qualities are. What things would you say you are acceptable at? Likewise, record these thoughts. We, as a whole, should be mindful of our qualities on the off chance that we need to accomplish a significant objective.

Build up an arrangement

Another pivotal piece of the procedure is the improvement of an unmistakable and obviously characterized arrangement. This will assist you with estimating and witness the advancement you are making, which thus will affirm your conviction that your endeavors are paying off. By following an arrangement, you figure out how to be reliably sheltered and create solid propensities.

The arrangement ought to depict your objectives. Begin conceptualizing about a rundown of things you figure you can't deal with serenely, yet plan to deal with effectively later on. These are your particular objectives. Include any accomplishments, even the ones that appear to be inconsequential. For instance, I felt a little awkward approaching outsider for bearings or help.

I needed to have the option to approach and talk unhesitatingly to everybody, and that is the reason I would add this to my rundown.

Try not to be hesitant to incorporate troublesome individuals, such as requesting advancement, giving a discourse in life with 1,000 individuals, or asking the young lady or the man in the corridor to go out to eat. Presently rank them from simple to troublesome and concentrate on achieving each before proceeding onward to another.

Every little accomplishment will give you an upgraded level of certainty that will assist you with drawing nearer and arrive at the following one. It will make these achievements from easy to difficult over time, and every time you achieve one, you will be rewarded, just like achieving a goal, knowing forever that you can do this. These little triumphs will never go away. They are steps on your way. Every time you move to a different goal, consider how you can apply your strengths to the situation to make it easier.

"Working smart is not difficult" still applies when possible. Work through each step until it's as comfortable as an old hat. By working on something sufficiently long and excelling, you will start to join these exercises into your life so that they become a propensity. They become simple. They begin to define you. To an important degree, you are what you do. Once you fully realize this concept, you begin to see that you really can become what you need to be. You make a move and start to characterize ourselves.

Now you are looking for information that tells me you are already putting this concept into practice, whether you knew it or not. It acts to define or redefine itself with more confidence. In a way, you are actually learning to be confident simply by taking action!

Commit to yourself

As you progress in your learning and begin to progress towards building your confidence, you will certainly encounter some obstacles. There will always be a small desire to stop, surrender, or avoid. Just remember that taking the easy path is like hiding challenges and breaking your trust instead of building. Whenever possible, stay committed to your personal growth and face challenges.

The best part is that even if you fail, you still gain confidence because you have faced the situation. Did you try! There is a lot of courage to find by simply facing fear or doubt and making an attempt.

You will probably find that doubt will always try to sneak in. But you will be looking for it. If these doubts arise, all you have to do is make a backup copy and investigate the situation objectively and realistically. Is this really possible? Do people do things like this all the time? If so, the chances are good that you can learn and do it too.

For example, at some point in a colleague's life, he was determined to go to medical school and become a doctor. He was a great student, already had a bachelor's degree, and many of the required courses had been completed. However, she was 35 years old and also had three children and no income. He started out determined and confident, but eventually, doubts arose about this journey.

The scrutiny told him that staying committed and confident could go a long way and helps his friends and family as much as possible, but borrowing 4-5 years and surviving without income before being able to return to work could prove to be more of a struggle than it was worth. The sorrow. Trying to deal with it while completing one of the most academically rigorous academic careers may not even be healthy.

You simply did not have a realistic and sustainable plan that suited your current situation.

Careful thought revealed that his motivation was strongly based on money and prestige, which could be a bad reason to drag his family through such difficulties. These accomplishments eventually led him to rethink this career as a viable option.

The moral of this is that not all doubts are irrational and based on fear, but many of them are. Be realistic in evaluating both your doubts and your goals. As you continue to learn to be confident, you will also learn to better assess your goals and fears.

Fortunately, some of these concepts will help you be better prepared as you continue on the path of building trust.

Keep this tip in mind and prepare yourself mentally as you continue your efforts to learn to be confident in all aspects of your life.

You will be more open and willing to accept any address you receive. Get ready and start finding your way to a new and safer one.

So, what should I do now?

Now you have some ideas on how to put your head in the right place, but to take your confidence to new heights, you need a plan and the will to follow it...

CONCLUSION

Fear is a normal human emotion, but very subjective. While normal fear has a beneficial and adaptive purpose, fear can also cause millions of people enormous suffering. From a biopsychosocial perspective, this article reviewed the starting point and practical motivation behind ordinary nervousness. The natural, mental, and social factors that add to the arrangement and support of (neurotic) nervousness issues were introduced.

The different tension issues, speculations, and related medicines were assessed. The treatment of nervousness issues depends on a strong logical premise in light of research by specialists from various fields. The examination researched these natural, social, and mental elements that add to the tension issues.

This broad research base has led to the development of numerous evidence-based treatments that have been shown to be highly effective.

As a result, thousands of brave people have regained their health, restored their function, and are now enjoying an enriching and rewarding life.

The future stays hopeful for the individuals who battle with dread. We are persuaded that progress in the treatment of tension issues will keep on giving expectations and help to people and families influenced by these disarranges.

The End

This book: STOP INSECURITY!

Build Resilience Improving your Self-Esteem and Self-Confidence! How to Live Confidently Overcoming Self-Doubt and Anxiety in Relationship, Insecurity in Love and Business Decision-Making

WRITTEN BY LEROY REYNOLDS

is geared towards providing exact and reliable information with regards to the topic and issue covered. The publication is sold with the idea that the publisher is not required to render accounting, officially permitted, or otherwise, qualified services. If advice is necessary, legal or professional, a practiced individual in the profession should be ordered.

against the publisher for any reparation, damages, or monetary loss due to the information herein, either directly or indirectly.

Respective authors own all copyrights not held by the publisher.

The information herein is offered for informational purposes solely, and is universal as so. The presentation of the information is without contract or any type of guarantee assurance.

The trademarks that are used are without any consent, and the publication of the trademark is without permission or backing by the trademark owner. All trademarks and brands within this book are for clarifying purposes only and are the owned by the owners themselves, not affiliated with this document.

CPSIA information can be obtained
at www.ICGtesting.com
Printed in the USA
LVHW081121300621
690925LV00048B/1112